Paradise NORTH
Seasons in the Upper Peninsula of Michigan

LON L. EMERICK

Paradise North

© 2010 Lon L. Emerick

All Illustrations & Photographs are copyrighted by and
all rights reserved to the artists credited:

William Hamilton, Mark Mitchell, Carolyn Damstra, Dean Premo,
Evan Premo, George Wanska, Lon Emerick, Lynn Emerick

LCCN 2010928738

ISBN: 978-0-965057-71-4

All rights reserved. Except for brief passages quoted as part of a review, no part of this book may be reproduced in any form or by any means without permission in writing from the publisher.

Book & Cover Design:
Salt River Graphics
Shepherd, Michigan

Limited Edition 2010

North Country Publishing
355 Heidtman Road
Skandia, MI 49885
1-866-942-7898
www.northcountrypublishing.com

Printed in the United States of America

This book was printed on FSC-certified paper,
with 10 percent recycled content.
Acid-free and ECF
(Elemental Chlorine Free)

FSC
Mixed Sources
Product group from well-managed forests, controlled sources and recycled wood or fiber
Cert no. BV-COC-023484
www.fsc.org
©1996 Forest Stewardship Council

Hahn Printing, Inc
Eagle River, Wisconsin

To: Thomas McKenney, Director
Bureau of Indian Affairs
19th Century

"I consider this whole region doomed to perpetual barrenness."

Contents

Winter

Wandering in Winter 7
The Joy of Wilderness 11
Birds of Winter 15
The Challenge of Predators 17
A Winter Picnic.............................. 21
Rock Kiln 27
Celts by the Inland Sea 29
The Sound of Silence 33

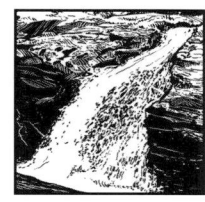

Summer

Cool, Clear Water...........................75
Keweenaw Magic 79
Goin' Camp 83
From Lake to Shining Lake 87
An Elegy for the Elm......................91
A Daughter of the Land 95
Investments in Summer 99
Legacy of the Land.......................103

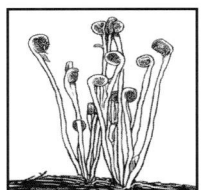

Spring

The Greening of the North 41
Symphony in the Forest 47
An Invitation to Spring 51
The Ponds 55
Historical Haywire Hike.................57
Dancing Cranes............................. 61
Roadside Treasures 63
The Flag Project.............................67

Autumn

In Praise of Goldenrod 113
Diamonds are Forever 115
The Golden Crown....................... 117
Chickadees on My Arrow............. 121
Discovering: The U.P. Anthem.....125
A Gathering in the Forest 129
The Gales of November 133
Old Farm...................................... 137

Epilogue: Pilgrim at Foster Creek 141
Code of the North: An Open Letter
    to Prospective Immigrants................. 147
APPENDICES
  A. Acknowledgments 151
  B. Photo Credits and Locations 153
  C. North Country Publishing Titles 155

Introduction

"There is no season such delight can bring as summer, autumn, winter and spring."

–Wm. Brown 1621

If you seek a superior place to visit, look north to a boreal paradise. Longtime residents of this lovely wild land have little yearning for heaven—we enjoy an Eden every day. Where else but in the Upper Peninsula of Michigan is there such an appealing blend of natural beauty, tangible history, ready opportunity for quiet and solitude and a unique and spirited group of human residents?

We live rich lives here, surrounded by the greatest lakes in North America. Rich not in material things but rather in a deep and abiding attachment to the land. We belong to the land and the land we belong to is grand. It is our paraphrased version of Camelot.

"If ever we could leave here, it couldn't be in springtime, summer, winter or fall, no, never could we leave here at all."

Each person fortunate enough to dwell in the Superior Peninsula may express attraction to the region in different ways. What lures and holds people to the Upper Peninsula may be spaciousness, beauty, remoteness, safety, uncrowded towns and landscapes, but especially the promise of quiet—the sound of silence.

Alas, the times they are a-changing. The Upper Peninsula has been discovered and the jarring noise and sight of development can be heard from every village green: trophy homes, condominiums, mining exploration, unseemly commercial sprawl. And will the new seekers who come here bring the values and expectations that transformed their old homes into places to flee? Will the power of our affection for this region allow us to retain a sense of place and a lifestyle we treasure amidst the forces of change?

Although much has been altered, much still abides. What we have here in our superior peninsula is good: Can we keep what we have? In my native valley there are many appealing features—rivers, lakes, marshes and vast forests are just a few. It is a privilege to walk in beauty every day. If we would continue to live in this wild and wonderful place, we must resolve to express our gratitude each day; to tread gently, with reverence and wonder; to maintain a lifestyle that will sustain this fragile boreal paradise for the generations that follow.

And so now I ask: Superior Land, how do I love thee? In the chapters that follow, let me count the ways.

Photo: Mark Mitchell

Winter

Mark Mitchell

Lon Emerick

Lon Emerick

4 WINTER

Winter
INTRODUCTION

An Upper Peninsula winter: It is the best of seasons, it is the worst of seasons. Actually, winter up here is not a season. It is an annual saga of endurance and survival. At least, that's what we want visitors to believe.

When summer tourists ask, always with a sly smile, how we cope with the glacial period, we paraphrase Lord Byron's grumpy appraisal of an English winter:

"A U.P. winter, ah yes, it ends in July only to recommence in August . . ."

Then, if the visitor continues to inquire about why we persist in living in a boreal clime, we exaggerate with a story like this:

One slow day at the Pearly Gates, St. Peter decided to amble down to Hell and see what the Devil was up to. There was a crowd of people waiting in line. Satan looked briefly at each one before tossing the doomed human into the flames. But once in a while, he carefully inspected an individual and then set them aside on a small bench. St. Peter asked, "Why do some people get put aside like that and not thrown into the fire?" "Oh," replied Satan, "Those are Yoopers. They are so wet and cold they won't burn."

The winters are long and cold up here. But we are very grateful for the interminable glacial interlude: If not for the snow, ice and frigid winds, land speculators and the rich and famous would buy up all the lakes, rivers and vast forests. So we don't tell outsiders that we like winter; it keeps out the riff-raff and weaklings addicted to comfort, convenience and a "climate."

The uncompromising northern winter offers a daily reminder that, despite all the efforts of modern technology to impose control over nature, there still are places that offer vivid challenges. Hence the gift of humility: the home place that makes us vulnerable to the forces of nature also makes us strong and independent. We cherish dwelling under a deep blue sky, breathing cold, zingy air and the exciting prospect of making it through a subzero spell or a storm that dumps 37 inches of wet snow in two days . . . in March! So we survive and thrive after the test of winters.

We agree with Anne Gradstreet, another Brit:

"If we had no winter, the spring would not be so pleasant."

WANDERING IN WINTER

There's a puzzle in the winter woods. Not crossword or Sudoko or how to locate a geo-cache. This puzzle is not made by man but by our other neighbors in the north country.

On a bright sunny day in January, a group of friends joined in a snowshoe trek through a snow-laden forest, across a small creek in black-and-white dress and out onto a frozen lake.

Not long into our adventure, we came across a set of distinct prints following a ridge line and then straight as a die out across the ice. Mary, who teaches winter ecology to NASA program participants, and Dean, co-owner of an environmental consulting firm, were our experts. "Wolf?" "Acts like one. The prints are almost large enough." "The straddle (space side to side between the track) doesn't seem wide enough for a wolf."

Once the prints could be scanned on the lighter snow cover of the lake, the answer was "coyote," hunting for a meal of small rodents or birds. Far down the lakeshore, under overhanging branches, we found the feathers and bones of a barred owl—the coyote probably didn't capture it, but may have made a meal here.

Meandering along the lake's frozen bays and inlets was another puzzle . . . much smaller prints. "Mink?" "Least weasel?" Following the tracks for some distance to a clearer spot, the consensus was that a mink had passed here in the night or early morning, just after the latest snow.

In our own home woods and waters south of Marquette, each snowshoe or ski trek is a chance to try to solve the puzzle of "Who was here last night while we slept?" We have many neighbors here—some we glimpse and others we never see except for the prints they leave behind.

The delicate tracery of a vole, prints barely denting the snow surface. A line of triangular shaped marks coming out of a snow bank and ending abruptly: a ruffed

GROUSE AND SQUIRREL TRACKS

grouse has come out of a nighttime bed and exploded abruptly into the air—that sound also startles us in the spring and fall.

Whitetail deer, stepping in a precise line as they search for winter food—one medium-sized print and one small one. The snow is deep and they sink with each step.

Why are they still in our woods when food is more abundant elsewhere and most of their companions have gone south?

Here are the tracks of snowshoe hares with comically long feet and impossibly long marks between jumps. They hole up under the low branches of the white pine where snow cover is light and the air is warmer. Squirrel tracks are everywhere, coming out of brush piles and fallen trees as they scamper along logs, up and down trees and across our paths.

Yesterday, the prints of a large canine crossed Heidtman Road, and stepped along our path up through the hemlock grove. We followed on the ridge, down into the valley and across a wetland. The track measured four-and-a-half inches long by three inches wide—hmm. We think it was a gray wolf, just passing through, but the uncertainty is what makes the winter woods puzzle game so much fun.

We usually puzzle over tracks made by unseen visitors. But rare sightings in our woods give us a match of prints and animal. Last year, a fisher bounded across our path in the east woods—dark glossy fur and long flowing tail. We got a clear look at its prints as we followed across ridges and old roads to the creek bank. Again, in December we watched from our living room as another fisher crossed the creek below us, climbed out of the valley, turned sideways to give us an excellent look at its distinctive face and retreated back to enjoy a morning meal.

Puzzling out the map of "who goes there" can add enjoyment in the winter woods. Several small guides can acquaint you with animal tracks. Two which will fit in your pocket or pack are *Animal Tracks of the Great Lakes* by Ian Sheldon and *Track Pack: Animal Tracks in Full Life Size* by Ed Gray. Another reference is *Animal Tracks and Signs of North America* by local author Richard P. Smith.

Before returning to a cozy fireplace and a cup of hot chocolate, take the time to scan the winter woods for other marvelous mysteries:

> The contours of the land are now clearly evident as the long shadows of winter drape the landscape in dreamy hues of blue. Is that long ridge an esker left by the last glacier?

> Look over there in that maple sapling—a bird's nest. How did we miss it through the summer? Was that where the chestnut-sided warbler raised a brood?

> Inspect the buds on the young maple carefully. Although they are folded tightly now, they are poised to respond to increased sunlight. Each bud is unique and each is a promise of new life, a promise of spring.

> Don't miss the beauty and mystery of snowflakes. Bring along a piece of black velvet cloth taped on a square of cardboard. A small hand lens or magnifying glass allows you to see the intricate shapes of the flakes. Wilson A. Bentley, (1865 -1931) a Jericho, Vermont farmer, devoted his lifetime to photographing snowflakes, Sadly, Mr. Bentley died in 1931 just before his now-famous book of photos was ready for distribution.

> Take time to have a conversation with trees. Look closely at the bark; I like to imagine each type of tree carries its personality here. Yellow birch bark looks like the tree has just had a permanent and it turned out very frizzy. Beech trees look so formal in their smooth gray bark . . . oh, look at that one: a bear has left its claw marks when it climbed high to harvest beech nuts.

> All living things prepare for winters by making adaptations to survive the cold. Both the willow gall midge and its host tree accommodate each other; the tree grows a protective shell—it looks like a pale green fuzzy pine cone—around the midge larvae, providing a snug winter home for the insect.

> In a feat of amazing engineering, mice and voles create extensive tunnels beneath the snow as protection from owls, foxes and weasels.

On a clear day in winter we can see so many things. Now with the foliage of summer just a nostalgic memory and the forest laid bare and open, we can appreciate the wonders revealed by our persistent glacial season. It will be months before the greening of the north; bundle up and saunter forth to witness the enduring patterns and mysteries of nature.

THE JOY OF WILDERNESS

Oh, what a beautiful morning. We are playing hooky to make our first visit to the ice caves in Alger County. The sun is low on the horizon and its rays ignite the glittering hoarfrost covering every weed and tree along the road.

We turn off M-94 East at Eben Junction. This wee hamlet was named for the brother of railroad superintendent Roscoe Young: Ebenezer Austin Young. Thankfully they abbreviated his name to Eben. The local punsters say that Eben is where old Finns go when they die.

By a sharp left curve on a snow-covered county road, we find the large open field described in our directions. Parking the car, we notice no one else is here. Following a well-packed trail through the deep snow, we enter a mature hardwood forest. Inspecting the huge maples, we see they were tapped in prior years to gather sap for making maple syrup. The long blue shadows on the snow are so dramatic we pause to savor the beauty and take a few photographs. We often stand still in the forest for our daily dose of serenity.

The trail spirals down to the edge of a deep ravine where in past years we discovered an old log cabin. The cabin is gone now but we stop to remember. Although the door hung open, it appeared as if the long-ago resident decided to leave suddenly one day; all his possessions were left behind. A blue and white wash basin, a rusty straight razor and a frayed towel were still aligned neatly on a small shelf. Who lived here and why did he leave so precipitously?

When we make the final turn on the trail, we again are not prepared for the gorgeous sight of the ice formations, situated in a large horseshoe-shaped cove, featuring a tall sandstone cliff. We marvel at the huge vertical sheets of ice; the long icicles are filigreed in many artful shapes by continual thawing and freezing as water drips over the ledge. We see hues of white, pale green and amber. Creeping between narrow openings in the ice sheets, we are overwhelmed by the eerie beauty inside the shallow caves.

At the present time, more than forty years after our first visit, the Eben ice caves are now included in the Rock River Canyon Wilderness, a 5,000 acre roadless, non-motorized area in the Hiawatha National Forest. After much delay and negotiation, the U.S. Forest Service recently acquired a 40-acre inholding—and now this entire area is safe from logging, road building and "development."

We have many wild places but not much true wilderness in the Upper Peninsula. Between two and three percent of the land has been set aside as roadless areas where humans are visitors but do not remain. Here is a partial listing of state and federal wilderness sites:

> STATE: Craig Lake State Park, located in the Michigamme Highlands in Baraga County; Porcupine Mountains Wilderness State Park, far western U.P. in Ontonagon County.

> FEDERAL: Beaver Basin in the Pictured Rocks National Lakeshore; Rock River Canyon, Big Island, Round Island and Horseshoe Bay in the Hiawatha National Forest; Sylvania Wilderness, Sturgeon River Gorge Wilderness and McCormick Wilderness Tract in the Ottawa National Forest.

There are opponents of the concept of wilderness and they are quite vocal in their dissent. Those who are willing to sacrifice anything for the bottom line see only waste in setting aside forest land which could be logged, mined or otherwise developed. Others believe that public land is being "locked up" and they resent any barriers to easy—read motorized—entry. "What of the elderly, the infirm?" ask the critics of wild places.

Elderly or physically challenged individuals rarely raise those objections; they realize that there are comparable sites they can visit and they want some wild and unchanged places for their children and grandchildren to explore. Most critics of roadless areas are men, often out of condition, who simply don't want to part with their dirt bikes, snowmobiles, ATVs or motorboats.

However, I suspect that the objections cited are only proximate reasons for a dislike of setting aside wilderness areas. The ultimate motivation for opposing wild areas is more visceral and involves fear and absence of control.

Consider the reactions of the first white men to behold this pristine continent. Their native lands had been deforested, tilled and tamed for a long time. They looked at the vast unbroken forests and, from somewhere deep in their psyches, saw only potential danger: wild Indians, wolves, bears, perhaps even evil spirits. So, what do you do when you perceive yourself as a small, insignificant cipher in a vast new world? Control. It was easy to be persuaded that one's well-being depended on a control of nature. Later came two other avenues of "c": the natural world must be managed for human *comfort* and *convenience*.

Perhaps it is time for the north country to have a vast yard sale and disencumber ourselves from archaic concepts about the natural world. Some business owners have already discovered an unexpected value in preserving wild places. Today, wilderness and wild areas have become a sustainable economic asset to the Upper Peninsula. Close proximity to wilderness is now advertised as a drawing card for visitors by some of the same people who opposed it.

Wild, free-growing places are as much a part of our heritage as libraries, art galleries and museums. Some cannot live happily without Mozart or Monet, opera or ballet. There are others who cannot live well without the solace of wild places. Robert Service spoke for those when he wrote:

> *"Thank God! There is always a Land of Beyond*
> *For us who are true to the trail;*
> *A vision to seek, a beckoning peak*
> *A fairness that will never fail."*

We return often to the ice caves in the Rock River Canyon Wilderness. Our favorite visits now are when we accompany friends who have not seen the icy creations of nature in winter. Then we can appreciate the frozen wonders again through the eyes of new visitors.

BIRDS OF WINTER

A pair of ravens lives on our Foster Creek Homestead (perhaps the birds see it differently and we live on the Raven Home Place).

In winter, they follow us about on our daily snowshoe soirees. Although they talk to each other in an extensive lexicon, this wild pair of ravens engages us only with "Here I am" quorks as we mush through the snowy forest.

Perhaps it is a meal the ravens are anticipating. We know they feast on red squirrels we leave here and there on stumps in the woods. These pesky little critters love to invade our log home; some population control is required to forestall illegal entries. So maybe the ravens see us as large predators; by sticking close to us on our rambles, they might be led to a winter picnic.

Bernd Heinrich, a wildlife biologist and raven doyen, has learned that ravens do in fact shadow wolves, coyotes and other predators in hopes of getting some leftovers (See Heinrich's *Mind of the Raven* and *Ravens in Winter*). His research revealed that ravens often try to alert predators to a road kill or carcass in the woods because carnivores are equipped to tear open the tough pelts of deer or other animals.

Members of the Corvid family—ravens, crows, jays—reportedly are the most intelligent of all bird species. Researchers have observed crows dropping small stones into partially-filled vessels, raising the water level so they could drink.

The Foster Creek ravens announce their arrival by a delightful swish-swish-swish of their wings sawing the still winter air. They land high in a maple tree, perch close together and utter a "tok" call as they touch beaks. They seem to have "names" for each other, a private vocalization reserved just for mates. They watch intently to determine which snowshoe trail we will take.

By early March, the raven pair will commence nesting and raising a family. Then they withdraw from any contact with the human dwellers of this land. We wish them well and respect their privacy; a squirrel or two will help to feed the young when they hatch.

Several other birds call the Foster Creek Homestead their place and also stay here all winter:

– *Ruffed Grouse*. These attractive game birds don't practice drumming during the winter months. On frigid winter nights they burrow into a snowdrift to stay "warm," at least warmer than in the open air. Researchers have found that light, fluffy snow makes good insulation; in the open it may be 15 degrees but a balmy 32 degrees or higher under the snow's surface. Grouse have a disconcerting habit of catapulting out of the snow almost under the tip of my snowshoes—the explosive sound is guaranteed to stop winter walkers in their tracks.

– *Barred Owl*. A pair of barred owls live somewhere along a densely wooded creek valley on the west border of the Homestead. They have the night shift so we rarely see them. On occasion we see the imprint of their wings, a drag mark and perhaps a bit of fur in the snow where they have taken a varying hare for their evening meal.

We do hear them serenading outside our bedroom window. They keep a hopeful vigil for rodents from the tall trees near the bird feeders. I listen carefully but so far they have never called my name (*I Hear the Owl call my Name* – Margaret Craven). The resident owls and pair of ravens have a tenuous truce. The ravens do not prey on the young owls in the nest and, as far as I can tell, the barred owls regard the ravens as neighbors and not dinner.

– *Black-capped chickadee*. What a lively and faithful year-round resident is this small bird. When I sally forth with a supply of sunflower seeds for our feeders, they land on my Stormy Kromer cap and call insistently for a snack. How do these little mites make it through the frigid nights?

Chickadees are the first birds to announce impending spring. Their clear whistle, "fee-bee-bee" reminds me that, even though March is cold and snowy, warmer weather is on the way. Wouldn't it be more appropriate to have the black-capped chickadee rather than the robin as the state bird of Michigan?

THE CHALLENGE OF PREDATORS

What a way to spoil a winter walk: Finding the carcasses of seven coyotes dumped in a ditch on a rural road. Among the bodies, we found some foam blocks used to identify animals entered into a predator challenge, along with a discarded memo prepared by the Huber Creek Rod and Gun Club. The title was Talking Points for the Predator Challenge.

The snow and rain had washed out the rest of the memo, but from our experience and comments heard during media interviews at various predator challenges, we imagined what those talking points would be:

COYOTES DUMPED BESIDE A RURAL ROAD

> "We have had complaints about our annual hunt for coyotes, fox and bobcats from 'animal rights' groups. Here are some things you can say in response. Remember, if you are talking from personal anecdotes and opinions, speak loudly and with great conviction.
>
> • Be vague in the use of numbers. Don't say coyotes or wolves killed 'seven' deer, say 'lots' were killed. When using anecdotes, don't use names. Say something like, 'A guy I work with has a cousin who knows a man in White Pine who found a bunch of deer killed by predators.'
>
> • Remind your listeners that predator hunters are the ones being harassed. They are trying to take away our guns, our Second

> Amendment rights; the DNR, in conspiracy with the auto insurance companies, brought in all these wolves at night in black helicopters; our hunting traditions are not being respected.
>
> • Describe the critics of organized predator hunting events as tree huggers, earth muffins, elitists, liberals. Hint broadly that what they really seek is creeping socialism or a completely vegan culture.
>
> • Finally, if the argument is raised that predators are an essential part of the balance of nature, dismiss it out-of-hand as some unproven theory of evolution. Remember that we approve of and want more of the good wildlife—deer, grouse, wild turkeys, snowshoe rabbits, etc. But we need to get rid of the bad wildlife—coyotes, wolves, cormorants, hawks and owls."

This clever, but unwise, portrait of hubris appeals to humans who are burdened with the belief that our single species has a manifest destiny to shape the natural world in any way we desire. We discovered that we could alter the ancient rhythms of nature and then we came to believe that nature exists solely for our control. We all live in our perceptions and thoughts and when these ideas are coded in language, repeated over and over ("predators are killing *our deer*") the slogans become truth and survive despite research and facts.

When I was preparing this chapter, I consulted a longtime deer hunter and asked him to read a draft. His response was quite blunt:

> "I experienced ups and downs in the deer population long before wolves and other animals became scapegoats and demons for unsuccessful hunters. Snow level seemed to be a factor, but deer populations tend to fluxuate.
>
> These complainers have themselves to blame, too. They put out piles of bait to attract deer. Deer tend to gather and hang out near the ready sources of food. Animals that prey on deer are then attracted to the crowd near the feeding sites. The deer then become wary and stay away from bait piles and the sedentary hunters waiting nearby."

I've tried to find some common ground with many disgruntled hunters, but their minds are made up. I read long ago that you can't reason someone out of a position they haven't reasoned themselves *into*. Many seem to believe that the fervor with which they hold an opinion, and the volume of their voices, determines the outcome of any controversy.

Why do these old attitudes about the natural world still linger? It is well-documented that populations of prey species—grouse and deer, for example—control predator numbers; nature worked out this dynamic balance long before humans began tinkering. All the animals—prey and predator alike—are part of a web, and the survival of the entire system depends on the well-being of each part. The evidence is clear: When we eliminate predators of deer, the deer population explodes and browses out their range in a short period of time.

Hunters in northern Arizona enjoyed good mule deer hunting in the early days of the twentieth century. Yet they wanted more—and saw predators as limiting their bag. They hired a Forest Service Warden. Warden Jim Owens was very good at his trade. He killed 554 bobcats, 781 mountain lions and 4,889 coyotes. The deer herd expanded dramatically and the hunters were ecstatic. Then came the crash. The deer got smaller as the herd grew, hungry animals destroyed their habitat and the deer population declined swiftly.

The very same experience was repeated in Pennsylvania, Michigan and Wisconsin. Is there a lesson here? When humans try to tinker with the ancient balance between prey and predators, nature's equilibrium tilts in ways that produce an unhappy and often unintended outcome.

It is painful to review our record as stewards of this pristine country: The bison were slaughtered; the old growth forest completely logged; passenger pigeons were hunted into extinction; beautiful wading birds like egrets were killed so that hats could have feather plumes—all results of our efforts to "man-age." Havelock Ellis summarized our avarice this way: "The sun and the moon and the stars would have disappeared long ago . . . had they happened to be within reach of predatory human hands."

Is it unreasonable to think we should have progressed enough to willingly share the planet with all creatures great and small? How did the natural world get by before we began to fulfill our destiny to manage everything?

We have no quarrel with a hunter matching wits with a wily coyote, nor certainly with sportsmen's clubs as places for improving marksmanship and hunting skills. But killing seven animals in a competitive event and dumping the carcasses beside the road, and another five found on a different road in the same township, is disrespectful and unethical. The individuals who did this cannot be called either hunters or sportsmen.

A WINTER PICNIC

The snow pack is at least three feet deep, the temperature hovers at 18 degrees—and the Sauntering Club has mushed into the forest by the Chocolay River for our monthly meeting and a noontime picnic.

We kindled a small fire on a granite overlook beside the river while Dick set up a portable table, covered it with a red and white cloth and lit a candle in a wine bottle. Sitting on our snowshoes, we feasted on grilled brats, raw veggies and a fruit scone. After a walkabout and plenty of fine and sometimes wild conversation, we adjourned the January meeting of the Thoreau Sauntering Club.

Henry David Thoreau was addicted to sauntering about his native Concord, Massachusetts. He described his sojourns in the forest as idle roaming in search of nature's secrets. Although the word "saunter" is of obscure origin, I have always preferred the Middle English version, "santren," which meant "to muse." We ponder freely as we roam about in a carefree manner.

THOREAU SAUNTERING CLUB LOGO

Our sauntering club has no dues, no bylaws, no rules or order. No minutes are kept—though some cynical observers consider that hours are being wasted—and we tolerate no rancor in our ranks. The monthly outings are planned around a ramble in the forest and usually include engaging discussions on a wide variety of topics.

The Sauntering Club was launched several years ago not long after I retired from university teaching. One night Thoreau came to me in a dream (maybe it was the anchovy pizza), stood at the foot of the bed with a look of wild surmise, and uttered this quote from his book *Walden*:

> "To affect the quality of a day, that is the highest of arts."

Even though I had many interests and was eager to pursue them, I pondered the vision. What did the quote from *Walden* have to do with me? Was it a warning? Some relatives of mine, and some close friends, alas, did not know what to do with their freedom when they retired. I remembered with some uneasiness one particular older man I passed almost every morning on my way to class. Just like clockwork, at exactly 8:00 a.m., he walked out of his house and stood uncertainly beside his garage; he seemed poised, as if ready to go to his office. He looked about querulously as if wondering what to do next, how to fill the enormous gap in his daily routine.

The members of the proposed Sauntering Club agreed that while we had enjoyed our work, and were good at it, it was time for a new and different chapter of our lives. We would explore our horizons both physically and mentally.

Having been physically active all our working lives, we knew better than to retire to the stereotypical rocking chair. Here was an opportunity to really explore this wondrous native valley, the Upper Peninsula of Michigan. We would strive (with John Muir) to be in our world, not just on it. Now that we had the time to saunter and savor the rocky hills, the extensive forests, the miles of Lake Superior shoreline, we would nourish our spirits by inspecting frozen waterfalls, and pay our annual respects to spring wildflowers and the autumn color spectacle. Following Emerson's advice, we would endeavor to be in harmony with nature: "*in the woods,*" he wrote, "*a man casts off his years, as the snake his slough, and at what period soever his life, is always a child. In the woods is perpetual youth.*"

Here are just a few of our adventures:

- Searching for spring bird migrants and local history during a walk through the ghost town of Morgan.
- Mountain biking in the newly dedicated Grand Island National Recreation Area.
- Retracing the footsteps of Native Americans and European explorers on the Bay de Noc hiking trail.

No sedentary life for us: We would postpone the inevitable hardening of our arteries as long as possible. Just as important to us, however, was avoiding mental inactivity with its associated dread disorder, "hardening of the categories." Curiosity is the one mental trait most linked with superior brain functioning over one's life span. We had witnessed too many people who became slothful of mind upon retirement and ended up as grumpy, opinionated old men. A questioning mind does not have room for crochets.

Now we had the leisure to enjoy adventures of the mind, to playfully explore ideas, issues, books. We would dig into local history, learn about maple syrup, identify the flora and fauna of our region. We would explore cultural and geographical diversity with vicarious excursions to Slovenia, Scotland, Switzerland, Greece and Antarctica through the eyes of fellow members who had been there.

Coincidentally, all members of the Thoreau Sauntering Club have so far been teachers, at various levels and in subjects ranging from English to social studies to geography. The diversity of backgrounds is an added and most welcome dimension that I had not thought about nor planned for at the outset.

I don't think any of us thought that we would have quite so much fun on our outings. The shared humor, insightful conversations and mutual support—the genuine camaraderie—are among the aspects we most treasure in the group.

We discovered, too, that adventures in the outdoors promote authenticity. There is little time or purpose in social posturing on a lengthy saunter in the forest. Sharing experiences in the woods encourages the shedding of defensive social armor and we can enjoy genuine relationships.

Finally, we found an unexpected bonus through our saunters: We rediscovered that there is a real difference between living in an area as simply a backdrop for your life, and that of feeling truly centered and in tune with your environment. Surrounded by the forests and granite hills, living near the myriad streams and lakes of our peninsula, we in the Sauntering Club feel connected to and in harmony with the earth.

How to Form an Outdoor Adventure Club

From time to time, especially when they see us having way too much fun, people have inquired about membership in our Sauntering Club. We always demur and suggest that nothing prevents them from creating their own organization. Usually, the response is a hesitant "I wouldn't know how." Suppressing a chuckle and a temptation to say, "Just go out and walk," we share a list of ideas:

It is always helpful, but not essential, to start with a maven, one person who is knowledgeable about the local area, someone who has a vision of the club's purpose, and is willing to initiate the scheduling procedures for monthly outings.

Start slowly, perhaps with asking two or three friends to go for a walk—nothing too organized in the beginning until you see how it goes. We limited our membership to five so that we could all be together in one vehicle when driving to some trailhead. This allows us to catch up socially, anticipate our saunter and process the event on the way home.

There is another important reason for limiting membership: the complexity of communication interactions increases exponentially with each new participant. Consider:

- a person alone has one communicative possibility
- two persons have two communicative possibilities (1 x 2 = 2)
- three persons (1 x 2 x 3 = 6)

Note how the possible communicative interactions increase with 4, 5 and 6 club members:

(1 x 2 x 3 x 4 = 24)

(1 x 2 x 3 x 4 x 5 = 120)

(1 x 2 x 3 x 4 x 5 x 6 = 820)

The club members must make a commitment to each other: when the monthly date for the outing is planned in advance, every effort must be made to attend. The scheduling process fragments badly when outings are on an ad hoc basis. Too much phoning back and forth to find a time when all can attend will lead to frustration.

Don't let inclement weather prevent an outing. Well, a wind chill well below zero or severe electrical storms do encourage rescheduling. But rain, snow? There is no bad weather, just inappropriate clothing.

It's the outing into the natural world which is the centerpiece of a sauntering club. Leave the rest of your lives at the trailhead (put them in the trunk of the car) and focus your senses on what's around you—the sights, aromas, sounds. Limit the chatter about things not present in the moment such as children, work, grandchildren, pending or past vacations, politics, etc.

Serendipity requires a mind set: it is not the destination but the journey that is important. When we are totally in the moment, we are open to pleasant surprises. To be sure, the Sauntering Club members have enjoyed reaching a waterfall, a sweeping vista on some headland, a remote ghost town. But most of the magic with which we have been blessed appeared unbidden along the way. It all depends on the observer's attitude.

It is wise to keep a journal and a photo album of the outdoor adventures you undertake. Memories are fleeting and we are all maturing inexorably. We joke that when we are in the "home" we can read our journal entries, scan the photos and relive our adventures (now almost 200 in number). Just be sure not to make the recording more important than the adventure itself.

Although not essential, we have made sweatshirts, polo shirts, hats, pens and even a large flag with our logo emblazoned on it. All this supports our mutual identity and, we have found, initiates some unique encounters with the public. We even have our own theme song composed by Rob Yuill, poet laureate of the club:

Song of the Saunterers
(To the tune of "Row, Row, Row, Your Boat")

Here we go a sauntering
o-ver the U. P.,
Strolling, talking, eating, too
it *suits* us to a "T."

Each *month* we take a different trip
to places known or not,
*Cau*tiously adventurous
we *give* each thing a shot.

Our *leader* knows just where to go
to *places* rarely seen,
He *searches* for that perfect spot -
a *place* to eat I mean.

In *saun*tering we eat of course
the *limit* is the sky,
We *try* to find at each locale
the *best* place for some pie.

When *soggy* is the path we tread
or *heat* begins to fry,
We keep our spirits bright & strong
and have a piece of pie.

Our *saunter* in mid-year is a
tria*thl*on of sorts,
The *last* leg is the hardest part,
to *eat* ice cream in shorts.

We'll *go* until we're doddering
and *hik*ing is a dream,
If *we* can't walk or ramble much,
we *still* can eat ice cream.

ROCK KILN

*L*et's take a stroll in the winter forest to the ghost village of Rock Kiln in western Alger County. Bring along skis or snowshoes, you might need them.

An interpretive sign provides some background on this village that flourished in the late 1880s. Just ahead is a long row of the remains of twelve huge kilns; here charcoal was prepared to fuel the blast furnaces smelting iron ore in Munising, Ishpeming and Negaunee.

In 1880, Hiram Burt of the Union Fuel Company hired Charles Schaffer to supervise the building of charcoal kilns at this and two other sites—the Laughing Whitefish River (near Deerton) and Glenwood (later called Onota) at the south end of Deer Lake. Born in Canada in 1845, Schaffer had an adventurous youth. He worked as a cowboy in Texas and after the Civil War broke out he joined the Union Army and marched through Georgia with Sherman's forces. In 1870, he came to Munising and worked in the iron smelting operations before he was hired by Burt. After the hardwood forests were depleted, he went into banking in Marquette. He served as the president of the Union National Bank from 1926 until his death at age 99 in 1943.

The first kiln attendants at Rock Kiln were French Canadians and Swedes; Albert Trombly was the head collier (tender of kilns) and Gustav Lindquist was hired as blacksmith. A large boarding house was built. Later in the brief operation here, many Finnish immigrants were hired to cut the hardwood that fueled the kilns. They chose to live south of the railroad line in a site that came to be known as Finn Hollow.

See the huge field just north of the kilns? That was where the workers piled the wood that fueled the charcoal kilns. Each kiln held an amazing thirty-five cords of hardwood; one acre of forest could yield thirty cords of wood. It took six to eight days to burn the wood slowly and another three days for it to cool enough so the workers could load charcoal into railroad cars. The life of a kiln attendant was challenging: heavy lifting, constant smoke and life-threatening tasks to monitor the burning. A collier had to climb up on a kiln to check for the appropriate amount of draft to ensure that the wood burned very slowly. There was always the danger of falling into the fire if the flimsy stone structure gave way under the worker's weight. Legend has it that one collier went missing and months later his charred bones were discovered when workers raked charcoal from one of the kilns.

By 1890, twenty railroad carloads of charcoal were produced in one month. At this rate of production the surrounding forest was rapidly stripped of available wood.

Look for the pipeline that brought water to the community from a large pond to the north. Scout around the east side of the large field for a long, low stone fence that supported the water pipe. An extensive water system was devised: a steam engine sited at the pond pumped water through the long pipeline to the village; later around 1889, a windmill took the place of the engine.

Children of the kiln workers went to school at Rock River, one mile to the east. Church services were also held at this small community which grew up around a lumber mill.

Life was harsh in the wilds of Alger County in the nineteenth century. A small cemetery is located to the east of the town site. Here you will find small wooden crosses marking the graves of three young girls, all daughters of the same family, who died of diphtheria in 1885.

A local group of volunteers—headed by Bea Anderson and John Parlin and assisted by the U.S. Forest Service and members of the Alger County Historical Society—is attempting to restore interpretive signs and stabilize at least one of the kilns. Last year they removed brushy tangles so the structures can be seen more easily.

Please treat this historical site with respect. Tread lightly and do not remove any artifacts from the old village. The people who lived, labored and died here so long ago deserve a full measure of our courtesy.

Directions to Rock Kiln

Travel M-28 East to Rock River Road (H-01) east of Shelter Bay. Turn south, cross the bridge over Rock River. At a sweeping left curve, go straight west on the Onota-Autrain Road. At about a quarter-mile, see a small Rock Kiln sign. Turn right, cross the old railroad bed. Follow the two-track road through the forest for about a mile; the road ends at a barrier of boulders. Walk a short distance to Rock Kiln. (It's also a fine walk or ski from the railroad bed to the site).

For more information about Rock Kiln, see the Daniel O'Rourke's Master's Thesis *Rock Kilns: A Case Study of Michigan's Charcoal Industry*, 1997. Michigan Technological University. A copy is on file at the Forest Service/Park Service Visitor Center in Munising.

CELTS BY THE INLAND SEA

We were not looking for a magical musical moment. All we sought was some respite from the oppressive heat one humid summer night. A walk at Marquette's Lower Harbor Park would do the trick. Lake Superior is a wonderful air conditioner.

Approaching the breakwall that extends into the lake and guards the harbor, we were startled to hear the keening skirl of Highland bagpipes playing *Scotland the Brave*.

When the piper finished there was a short pause and then, from somewhere farther out on the massive concrete spit, came the distinctive notes of *Forty Shades of Green* played on an Irish pennywhistle. When the whistle went silent, the piper responded with a lively version of the Scottish tune *Skye Boat Song*. The musician with the pennywhistle countered with a plaintive version of *Danny Boy* that brought tears to our eyes.

"Dueling Celts," murmured Lynn in the silence which followed a spontaneous burst of applause from several other sleepless residents who had reveled in the impromptu concert.

Over the past decade there has emerged a cottage industry devoted to all things Celtic: graphic art; jewelry, especially Celtic crosses and brooches in classic loops and knots; music and literature. If you visit Sedona, Arizona, you will find New Age Celts wearing white robes and dancing around stone circles in the red rock canyons.

Who were the ancient Celts (the Greeks called them *Keltoi* and the word Celt is pronounced with a "k" sound) and where do their descendants live now? The Celts were a related group of tribes that lived and thrived in Northern Europe during the era of the Roman Empire. An innovative, artistic and energetic people, they pioneered the use of iron for making tools and weapons; invented chain armor; were the first to shoe horses; created stone shrines and built elaborate stone fortifications on rocky hilltops.

When the Roman Legions pushed the Celts out of Europe and then invaded the British Isles, the Celtic tribes fled westward to rocky redoubts in Cornwall, Ireland, Scotland and Wales that the invaders deemed worthless or militarily untenable. The Romans—as did later invaders of Britain—feared and despised the Celts. They wanted nothing to do with fierce Celtic warriors who painted themselves blue and went naked into battle.

There are six Celtic countries or sections of countries. We have just mentioned four: Scotland, Ireland, Wales and Cornwall. Can you name the other two? *

People of Celtic ancestry share some traits in common: a tendency to be intuitive, even impulsive; determinedly independent but also fiercely loyal; a unique blend of mirth and melancholy; a love of flowery language; astonishing visual artistry; and an abiding, almost mystical connection to the natural world.

Doesn't that sound like many residents of the Upper Peninsula? Indeed, many Irish, Cornish, Welsh and Scots came here to work in the copper and iron mines during the boom years. Their descendants are still here. They flock to concerts by *Boys of the Lough* and the *Battlefield Band*, and to Cornish reunions in Calumet. During a fund-raising drive for public radio, one old Celt even offered to paint himself blue and scale the Cohodas Administrative Building at Northern Michigan University to inspire contributions. Cooler heads prevailed.

You have a chance to celebrate a Celtic holiday on January 25, the annual celebration of the birth date of Robert Burns (1759-1796), the national poet of Scotland. Many of us with Celtic ancestry host a party; Scots call them *ceilidhs* (pronounced *kay-lee*) with music, dancing and a feast. The least you can do is eat a scone; amuse the clerk at the bakery by using the proper Scottish pronunciation, *skahn*. Skip the haggis.

The Cornish brought some distinctive food, in addition to the pasty, with them when they immigrated to America.

Can you solve this culinary quiz?

- You won't find this edible substance on the open shelves of local grocery stores.
- You must ask for it at the service counter and then pay immediately, not at the checkout aisles.
- It is expensive: A pound would cost more than $4,000.
- Romans used the substance to curdle cheese and dye clothing.
- One small duchy in Britain reportedly consumes twenty percent of the annual crop.
- There is a U.P. connection.

So, what is it? The correct answer is *saffron*. Saffron is a deep orange, aromatic and pungent spice used to color and flavor food—historically it was used as a dye and for medicinal purposes. It comes from the dried stamens of a crocus flower (*crocus sativus*), which only grows well in the Mediterranean region. It takes 4,300 blossoms to produce an ounce of the spice. And all the collection work is done by hand.

Cornish miners brought saffron with them when they immigrated to the Upper Peninsula in the mid-1800s. The spice has been an important part of Cornish culture since it was introduced by Phoenician mariners as barter for Cornwall's abundant tin. The miners just had to have the tasty yellow buns and bread—even if they were costly. There is a Cornish expression that my maternal grandmother repeated often: "As dear as saffron."

That's probably why Grandmother insisted that non-Cornish guests sample a small slice of saffron cake before she served them an entire portion. Some people are repelled by the flavor of the spice—the most candid guests (including my non-Cornish father and my Scots-Irish wife) say it tastes medicinal—like iodine.

I forgot the family taste-test and offered some fresh saffron buns to participants on a winter hike. On the return trek, I noticed small golden flakes in the snow where a shy hiker had crumbled and discarded his slice. I smiled as Grandmother's image flashed into my memory.

SAFFRON FLOWER

One doesn't have to be Cornish to enjoy a saffron bun—but it helps. Yet men must be careful, according to Jean Ellis, a Cornish Bard who resides in Eagle Harbor: "When saffron is combined with testosterone, you never know what may happen."

By the way, St. Piran's Feast Day is March 5. It is a good time to eat a pasty or a saffron bun in memory of Cornwall's patron saint. You can find good saffron buns and bread at several places in the Upper Peninsula. As you might expect, the most memorable locations are in the Copper Country—Toni's Country Kitchen and Bakery in Laurium, Slim's Café in Mohawk, and a real Cornish establishment, Jack and Carol Treganowan's Eagle River Country Store (look here for the flag of Cornwall, a white cross on a black field). Or if you're in Marquette you may be able to score saffron buns at the Marquette Baking Company on Baraga Avenue.

The Irish and the Cornish were also noted for their bloody battles. No doubt liquor was involved, as well as the volatile Celtic propensities of both ethnic groups, but most of the animosity stemmed from the fact the lads from Cornwall were expert miners. While the *Cousin Jack*s were performing tasks that called for hard rock mining skills, the Irish were relegated to menial labor. All was forgotten on St. Patrick's Day, March 17. After the traditional parade, a feast of Irish stew and soda bread, the drinking started. It was every Celt for himself when the whiskey and beer ran out.

I leave you with David Yeadon's Celtic Blessing:

> *"May the trees of the forest take root in your heart that you may grow in wisdom, joy and love for all who live in the Earth's embrace."*

* The Isle of Man (Manx) and Brittany (Bretons) in France.

THE SOUND OF SILENCE

At a gathering of contented Upper Peninsula residents, we asked that each person describe his or her attraction to life here in one-word responses. Since most of our friends are quite used to our philosophical—and sometimes rather odd—approaches to conversation, there were a few moments of silence and then they dove right in. The list included: space, beauty, remote, clean, safe, uncrowded, even cold(!) But one adjective kept emerging: *Quiet*.

It takes considerable coaxing to uproot me from this northern paradise; when I am away from my native valley for very long, I am a morose sojourner. Overwhelmed by the incessant activity in more populous places, I seek a path less traveled and focus on the advice of e.e. cummings: When the world of *made* is too much with me, I head for the world of *born*. The medication I need is a quiet haven—the doses are free and, while habit-forming, include no untoward side effects and are sure to produce serenity. *Quiet* – How sweet the absence of noise that soothes a woods walker like me! Living up here, or visiting in the U.P., offers opportunities to savor the sound of silence. We know that intimately. Since we moved to our home in the woods of West Branch Township over fifteen years ago, we have remarked often that the quiet at night is so complete and profound that it almost has a sound of its own—sort of a deep murmuring hum.

Background noise—which all of us have in our daily lives—is one common source of stress. Even when not consciously perceived, noise has been related to increased blood pressure and adrenalin levels, as well as general tension, irritability and insomnia.

Man-made noise also has an effect on wildlife: higher levels of stress (there's that word again), prey that can't hear approaching predators, even interruption in echolocation for animals which use reflected sound for navigation.

"We dwell in a world of noise...open a window, anytime, anywhere, and you'll hear the clamor . . . Increasingly, even wild places are

noisy with powerboats, jet skis, snowmobiles, trail bikes and ATVs . . . the silences of wild places are not yet gone, but they are vanishing."

—Jack Kulpa, True North—Reflections on Fishing and a Life Well Lived

Eight years ago, the National Park Service established a "natural sounds" department in Fort Collins (Colorado). Its main task is preserving "soundscapes," or places where visitors can "rest their ears." Several national parks and monuments have been identified as among the quietest, including one in our own backyard: Isle Royale National Park. Others are Great Basin in Nevada, North Cascades in Washington and Big Hole National Battlefield in Montana.

Some people object—usually quite loudly—that policies designed to promote quiet places are discriminatory, that it is unfair to lock them and their motorized sports out of public property. Such multiple use, however, is incompatible with visitors entering remote areas by silent means. Seven cross-country skiers, hikers and snowshoes can enjoy an area with minimal impact on the land or on others. One snowmobile or ATV can be heard and smelled for a long way.

A fellow saunterer endorses the idea of having one or two large theme parks where those addicted to outdoor activities involving speed and noise can gather to satisfy their needs. There could be race tracks for snowmobiles, ATVs, dirt bikes; glades where the future hearing-impaired could crank up their boom boxes and have parties; places for those who like to play cops and robbers with paint ball weapons. Then, since the remainder of the Upper Peninsula would be off-limits to these pursuits, the rest of us could revel in the quiet.

It's not all about the simple pursuit of silence. By quiet, we don't mean—nor does the Park Service—the absence of all sounds. Natural sounds can be an important part of an outdoor experience. Many of us are soothed by the sound of waves, thrilled by the rumble of a waterfall, delighted at the song of the Hermit Thrush on a spring morning and comforted by the distinctive sound of wind in the white pines.

It certainly is possible to become addicted to noise. Some people find the quiet of the Upper Peninsula to be ominous and disturbing. Coming into our more remote areas from the background noise of the city, they become anxious, saying they are not used to and don't know how to be alone and quiet. They often try to dampen down those anxious feelings by lots of activity and lots of talk.

Which brings us to the concept that, in addition to external human-created noise, which stresses some and may comfort others, there also is internal noise—inner chaff that we carry with us. We can't say it any better than did Henry David Thoreau, more than 150 years ago:

"I feel a little alarmed when it happens that I have walked a mile into the woods bodily, without getting there in spirit. I would fain

forget all my morning's occupation, my obligations to society. But sometimes it happens that I cannot easily shake off the village: the thought of some work, some surveying, will run in my head, and I am not where my body is. I am out of my senses. "In my walks, I would return to my senses like a bird or a beast. What business have I in the woods, if I am thinking of something out of the woods?"

—HDT, November 25, 1850

Stilling the inner voice is not easy. It can be achieved by allowing events to pass over you as raw sensations. Focus on your senses: feel the soft breeze on your face; listen for the rustle of leaves; admire the delicate play of light and shadow under the trees; smell the musty herbal essence rising from the forest floor; nibble on a blade of grass or tree bud.

The key is to be present in the moment. In her book *Dawn Light*, Dawn Ackerman offers this reward: "Presence is always a gift . . . waiting to be unwrapped and explored." *

The most magical moments we have in the outdoors arrive unexpectedly when we simply wait quietly with an open heart.

Inspired by Gorden Hampton's book *One Square Inch of Silence*, I have created a six-foot circle of silence at our Foster Creek Homestead. The circle is located in a dense hardwood forest near the southern edge of our property; it is guarded by high ridges and sited close to a lofty sugar maple tree that probably was a sapling when Gifford Pinchot started the U.S. Forest Service in the first decade of the twentieth century.

A cairn of local stones and six cordwood seats are the only adornments. I come here often to listen to the stirring of the leaves or the haunting melody of a white-throated sparrow. My sound level meter reveals an extraordinarily low measure of 27 decibels.

Do you have a favorite spot . . . a woodlot, old farm field, backwoods ski or snowshoe trail, a cabin deep in the forest, a granite overlook, wild Superior beach? Leave your other world, with its noise, cares and talk, at the parking lot or trailhead. Immerse yourself in the natural world which surrounds us here. Wisdom comes from being still. Go quietly.

* In your own search for the gifts of silence, you may find valuable hints in these books to guide you: *Dawn Light* by Diane Ackerman, *A Book of Silence* by Sara Maitland, *Listening Below the Noise* by Anne LeClaire.

Photo: Lon Emerick

Spring

Lon Emerick

Lynn Emerick

Lynn Emerick

Lon Emerick

38 SPRING

Spring
INTRODUCTION

There is no way people who live in San Diego, Tucson or Tampa can understand why residents of the Upper Peninsula greet minor signs of spring with such ecstasy. Only if you have lived through a five-month glacial season can you appreciate our joy at seeing melting snow, longer days of sunshine and, most thrilling of all, the first hint of green showing in the fields and forest.

Early or delayed, brief or extended, spring is a magical season in our northern paradise. We become excited and restless to be rid of the cocoon of winter; there is a compelling urge to go on a pilgrimage of sorts to witness every sign of renewed life. No wonder our forebears celebrated the vernal equinox.

My Celtic ancestors knew how to celebrate the arrival of spring. They built bonfires on the rocky headlands of Cornwall and offered prayers to Easter, the goddess of spring and fertility (Easter's totem animal was a hare, perhaps the original Easter bunny). They were especially awed by moving water—"running water is a holy thing" is a Celtic epigram.

In Cornwall they still celebrate "Dipping Day." On May 1 it is permissible to sprinkle water on anyone who is not wearing a sprig of new green taken from a hawthorn tree. Now I know why my Cornish relatives wore a sprig of cedar pinned to their garments on May Day.

Spring in these environs is ephemeral. There is a very noticeable tug-of-war between cold and warm from late March clear into May; winter does not go gently into the extended sunlight. One May a friend and I had planned a reconnoiter for a hike he was leading for the local Life Long Learning organization. Dick and I were exploring the southern end of the Big Island Wilderness in Alger County. The area features several remote lakes and old growth forest; it is a good place to see early spring wildflowers. On the morning of our sojourn, a light snow was falling. Undeterred, we sallied forth into the Hiawatha National Forest. And, were we glad we did! The forest was magical: the wildflowers—spring beauty, hepatica, adder's tongue—all were rimmed with fluffy white and their colors were more vivid than usual against the snow. The woods were quiet, dark and deep and the lakes were gorgeous against the light covering of white. Neither of us, despite living in this northern paradise for many years, had experienced so vividly the seasons dancing and jousting with each other.

If we are patient, as we must be, the ecstasy of spring arrives to stay. Nature seems to pick up speed to get the vast stage ready for the next act: Summer. One morning the phoebes arrive, then the winter wren starts its winter concert near Foster Creek. Then—oh the joy—we are awakened by a night chorus of spring peepers. We've made it through the winter!

THE GREENING OF THE NORTH

Each autumn, the "leaf-lookers" come north to see the extravaganza nature creates in the forests: Maples, aspen and birches on every hillside pulsate in brilliant hues of yellow, scarlet and orange. The annual display is so intense, so spectacular, that it overwhelms even long time residents.

Yet there is another, less well-known, color display which unfolds gently each spring. The show is more subtle, more delicate than autumn's spectacle, but residents of the north know that the soft spread of green across the hills heralds the end of the long winter season.

It's difficult for people who live in warmer climes to understand why spring is a major— indeed magical—event in the north. The joy of open water, a bare sun-warmed hillside, or the first wildflower cannot be truly appreciated simply by coming north for the spring.

After living through an extended winter, enduring the many storms, the short twilight days and the weeks of frigid arctic air, it becomes terribly important to find some evidence of new life: snowmelt around the trunk of a birch tree; a clump of willows wearing a new tiara of soft gray buds; the faint scent of trailing arbutus in bloom.

For those of us addicted to the many charms of spring, these early transformations are an epiphany. The sun brings a warming to the human spirit as well as to the land.

While many are called to the autumnal display, only a few choose to celebrate the first fleeting wonders of nature's renewal. Unlike the bold splashes of color which announce the arrival of fall, the spring color display is understated, subdued and very delicate. The new leaves unfold in pastel hues. It looks as if an artist had dipped a giant brush into several shades of green and touched the hillsides softly, hesitantly. Vast stands of dark pine and spruce punctuate and highlight the harmonious mixture of soft green. Add a cobalt sky and the immense blue of Lake Superior and you have a visual delight for winter-weary eyes.

The greening of the north generally occurs from early to mid-May. But spring in this region can be fickle, so prepare for a wide range of temperatures. The seasons jostle each other and weather conditions vacillate from one extreme to the other. Spring is often wet as well as changeable, but those prepared for outdoor excursions will discover that the greens take on even more nuances of color when misted. And the smells of the unfolding leaves and growing forest floor after a shower are lovely perfumes.

You will be able to see the sweep of spring color almost anywhere in the hills and valleys of the Upper Peninsula, but it is in the central and western regions where viewing is most spectacular. The drive from Marquette to Copper Harbor, especially up and over Brockway Mountain Drive, is one of the favorites. Follow U.S. 41 through Champion, L'Anse and Houghton. Many travelers like a view on M-107 from Silver City to the escarpment in Porcupine Wilderness State Park. Another good spot for observing the spring green is the stretch of U.S. 2 from Iron River to Watersmeet.

If you make the university town of Marquette your base, check out these short drives:

- County Road 492 from M-35 east past the old Morgan Heights area to Grove Street.
- County Road 480 from the intersection with County Road 553 and west to M-35.
- M-35 from County Road 480 to Palmer, especially the hills by GooseLake.

Remember to drive carefully on these winding, two lane roads. The deer, too, will be out looking for the color green—the grass beside the highway.

We also like to see nature's reaffirmation of life on foot, slowly. While you are walking, take time to scan the forest floor. You may spot a wildflower or find ferns unfolding, fiddleheads nodding together in the sunshine like ancient druids. The best times of day for viewing the spring colors are early morning and evening after 3:00 p.m.

Why don't you join us on a journey to a new place and revel in the green renewal of the north? On this excursion we will head to the eastern part of the Upper Peninsula; we will even spend some time in Paradise. Literally.

The drive east on M-28 to Hulbert is very pleasant. We pass through the small towns of Shingleton, Seney, McMillan and other barely discernible spots on the highway where short-lived villages died without names. The high ridges just east of Seney are stunning in many shades of soft green.

We plan to stay the night at Hulbert Lake Lodge. There are many places in the area that cater to travelers but we know the owner, Marge Curtis, and always enjoy the comfort and quiet in cabins overlooking Hulbert Lake.

At breakfast, be sure to ask Marge about the history of Hulbert Lake. She knows this area well and will be pleased to show you a book of photographs and share local lore.

Hoka hay! It is a good day to dawdle. We proceed east, still on M-28, to Brimley. Turn north here on Lake Shore Drive (221) and go past Bay Mills to join an extension of the same road, now designated as the Curley Lewis Memorial Scenic Lakeshore Drive. Go slowly because this twenty-mile roadway offers many delights to the traveler who will mosey along.

Our first stop will be at the Point Iroquois Lighthouse. Established in 1844 to alert ships of Lake Superior's dangerous reefs, the lighthouse has been restored as a museum. In season, you can climb the tower for a spectacular view of the lake. Even better, saunter along the boardwalk to the shore so that you can see, smell, hear and touch the Big Lake up close and personal. You might even find an agate on this beach.

Be sure to stop and explore the Big Pines Picnic area. It really does feature large white pines and a very appealing stretch of sand beach.

The North Country Trail winds along beside Lake Superior on the north side of the scenic highway. Our favorite spot for a saunter on this part of the Trail is just past Naomikong Point and a river of the same name. There is a very pleasant walk to a newly constructed bridge over the Naomikong; this is a good place to see the new green growth in the wetlands close to the river.

The scenic roadway ends at M-123. Turn north and head for Paradise. First, though, stop and admire the dark water of the Tahquamenon River at the Rivermouth section of the state park. Logging was a huge enterprise here in the late 1800s.

Paradise! An appropriate name for a village in the forest beside Lake Superior. Now it's lunchtime and we *must* go to the Berry Patch Café to see Shirley and get a piece of her world-class blueberry pie. We always feel like family here.

Lynn and I are nicely tucked into our pie and having a good time catching up with Shirley Clark when paradise is shattered by a very large, blustering and

MASTER PIE MAKER SHIRLEY CLARK

opinionated tourist. The tall troll had barely squeezed in through the door when he began hollering: "YOU HAVE ANY FOOD IN THIS JOINT? IS IT ANY GOOD? HOW LONG DOES IT TAKE TO GET SERVICE HERE?" His two companions, obviously embarrassed, rolled their eyes and shrugged.

The proclamations continued. Pretending to talk to his companions, the loud-mouth brayed, "WHAT A JERKWATER TOWN. DO PEOPLE REALLY LIVE HERE? PEOPLE WHO ARE REALLY WITH IT LIVE DOWNSTATE. THE WHOLE AREA IS WASTED ON YOOPERS, ANYWAY."

I will spare the reader more of the diatribe. But I could not contain myself. Clearing my throat, I said, "Yes, the U.P. is cold and backward—you wouldn't like it here. But, you know, if you keep talking like that, Yoopers will take offense and there are lots of places to hide bodies up here, even as large as yours."

The troll turns his chair toward our table where I sat with Lynn and Shirley. "WHAT IS THIS?" he shouted, pointed at us, "THE LADIES AID SOCIETY MEETING?"

As we rose to leave, I came over to his table and in a soft, measured voice, asked, "What is there missing in your life that you behave like this?" Not waiting for a reply, I left the café. Before I went out the door, however, I glanced back at an elderly man eating alone at a corner table. He smiled and gave me a thumbs-up.

As chance would have it, the following year we again happened to be enjoying pie in the Berry Patch at the same time as the local man who had given silent approval for my comments to last year's loud tourist. He came over to our table and told us this tale:

> *Word around Paradise was that the abusive troll died very soon after our encounter in the restaurant. Against advice, he insisted on climbing the tower at the Point Iroquois Lighthouse. The word is that he got wedged somewhere in the spiral staircase, went into a hissy fit and expired. At great effort, his body was taken to Newberry. The mortician could not find a casket big enough for the man. Showing Yooper ingenuity, the mortician let all the hot air out of his deceased client. When he finished, the remains were so small, they fit into a shoebox.*

Well, so much for northern tales. Most tourists who come to the U.P. are very pleasant. We are happy to see them—and happy to see them leave.

Let's return to our journey into spring. After lunch, we head north to Whitefish Point. Here you can observe biologists collecting data on the thousands of birds that use this point as a resting area for the annual migrations. The Great Lakes Shipwreck Museum here is also worth a visit.

Onward. Returning to M-123, we now drive westward to visit the lower and upper falls of the Tahquamenon River. There are short trails at both locations and a lovely quiet four-mile pathway between the two falls along the river and through the wildflowers. As a fitting end to a day of discovery, plan to have dinner at the Tahquamenon Brewery and Pub. Make a toast to the abundant wonders we are privileged to enjoy in our Northern Paradise.

But don't hesitate or wait too long to explore, for spring is fleeting in our native valley. Nature seems to realize that time is very limited—every moment of sunshine is important. Suddenly one day, all the deciduous trees are dark green and each aspen, maple and birch is going about the business of photosynthesis as quickly as possible. Full summer is coming to the north. The slide toward autumn has already begun. But we have caught and kept the memories of another spring.

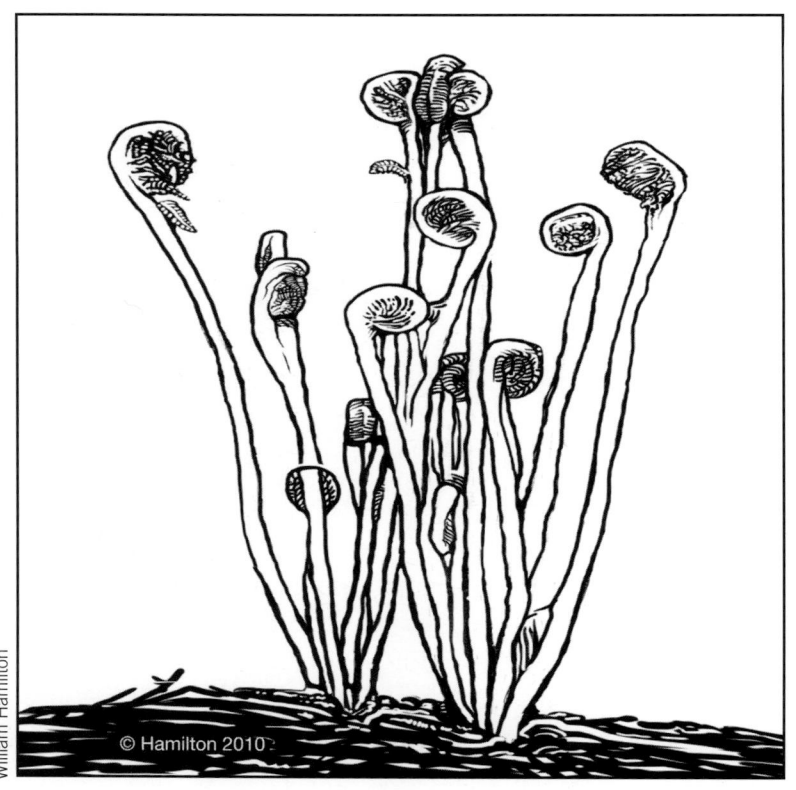

William Hamilton

SYMPHONY IN THE FOREST

If you would like to attend a free concert in the forest and see birds up close and personal, make plans now to visit the AuTrain Songbird Trail this spring. This one-of-a-kind nature trail is located in the Hiawatha National Forest, west of Munising in the north-central area of the Upper Peninsula. The first of its kind anywhere, the interpretive trail offers visitors an opportunity to actually carry on a dialogue with red-winged blackbirds, winter wrens and 18 other species of birds.

Located at the AuTrain campground, the Songbird Trail was developed as a cooperative project by the U.S. Forest Service, AuTrain Visitors Association, Michigan Department of Natural Resources and several volunteers.

To find the trail, follow H-03 (known locally as the Forest Lake Road) to Forest Service Road 2276 where signs will direct you to the campground. Take the campsite loop on the right and look for the big sign marking the trailhead. The trail is open all day, but the best time for enjoying a woodland concert is in the morning when the singers are the most active. The two-mile path is well marked with blue diamonds and easy to follow. Posters with illustrations and descriptions of each bird are located strategically along the trail where walkers are most likely to encounter the bird.

There is also a kit containing a bird identification manual, binoculars and a tape recorder with a prepared cassette. The kits are available at A&L grocery or AuTrain grocery in AuTrain or from the campground host. There is a deposit to rent the kit and most of the deposit is refunded when the kit is returned. While it is possible to walk the trail without the accompanying kit, the experience is greatly enhanced with the audiovisual material.

The tape recording guides you along the trail. The visitor stops at each observation site—designated by posters of the twenty birds—and plays the tape. Each bird and its unique song is described. Here is a portion of the narrative describing the song of the winter wren:

Surely someone must be practicing Mozart's *Nachtmusik* in the damp thickets beside Buck Bay Creek! The song of the winter wren is a series of silver notes which seem to tumble and tinkle, slow, and then swell and resume their delightful cadence.

Each bird's song is also on the cassette to assist in identification. Many birds respond readily to the tape and will come close to investigate. Last June a visitor reported that a veery, a small thrush, actually flew in and pecked at the recorder which had been placed on a nearby stump.

Even if the trail were not an excellent area for seeing birds—as many as 100 different species have been spotted there—it would be a very pleasant place for a walk in the woods. Here are some things to look for during your visit:

- Walk down to the shore of Buck Bay and climb an observation platform for a stunning view. You may spot ducks, shore birds, maybe a heron. Both a bald eagle and an osprey frequent this spot.

- Look for wildflowers where the trail winds beside Buck Bay Creek. Take time to sit on one of the benches and listen to the melody of the water as the creek surges toward AuTrain Lake.

- At the midway point, where the trail emerges into a small clearing, see if you can find any remnants of an old logging camp. Please don't take any items away.

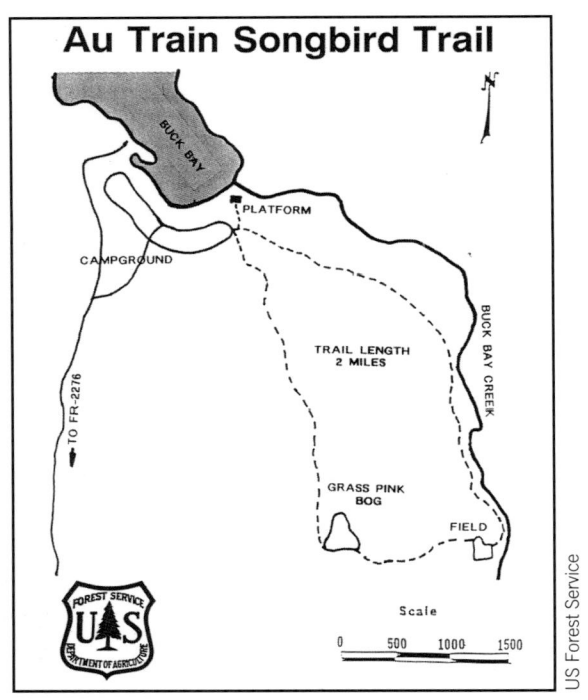

AUTRAIN SONGBIRD TRAIL MAP

- Pause and admire the Grass Pink bog. Here, eons ago, a glacier dropped an immense chunk of ice. The resulting small pond has long-since filled in with lush moss and small trees. In June, the beautiful pink orchid blooms here.

- As the trail turns back toward the campground, note the many fine maple, cherry and beech trees. Look carefully at the smooth gray beech trees; on some you will see the clear claw marks made by a black bear while climbing aloft for beechnuts.

While not strenuous, the Songbird Trail winds over uneven ground, exposed roots and a few wet spots. Since birds time their arrival here to coincide with the annual insect invasion, be prepared with clothing and repellent.

So come and enjoy a wonderful medley of songs performed by colorful singers. The stage will be trimmed in shades of green and a myriad of wildflowers will serve as the backdrop. Enjoy the show!

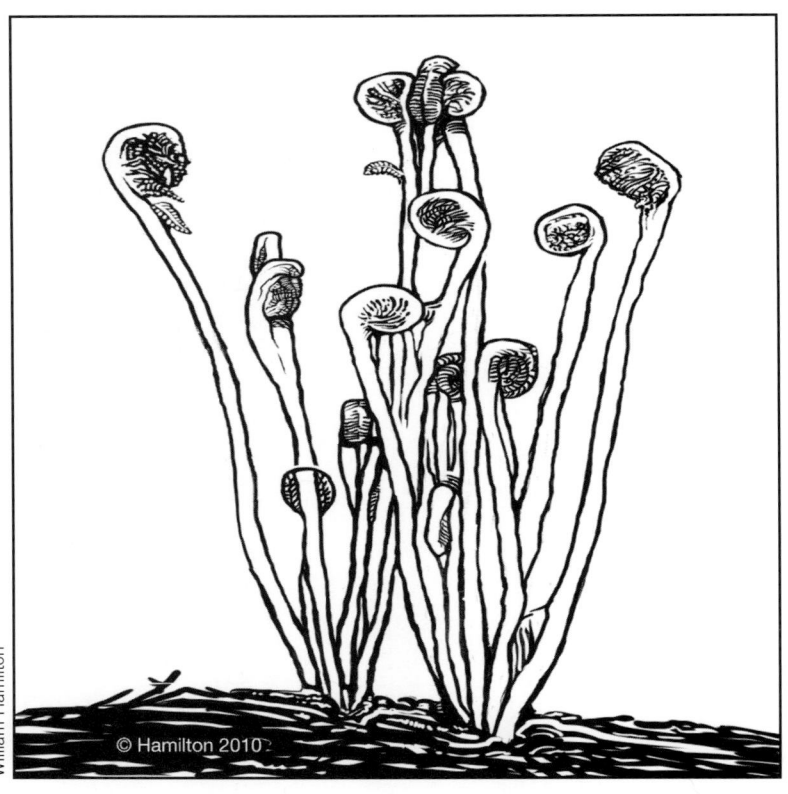

William Hamilton

AN INVITATION TO SPRING

There has always been one day each spring that epitomizes the season for me, one special day in which the forces converge in a unique essence of change and a new beginning.

Today, May 10, is such a day. It is 8:00 a.m., and I am standing on the shore of McKeever Lake in the Hiawatha National Forest waiting for the participants in a nature walk I will lead.

A long time ago, a favorite professor of mine used this elegant phrase to describe a similar spring day: "Everything is a verb in May."

The urgency of the new season is unmistakable. Nature seems to realize that time is very short in the North Country and that much of the colorful bounty must unfold swiftly. Every hour of sunshine is precious. There is no time to linger.

McKeever Lake is glistening in the slanting rays of the morning sun and the hills on the far shore are aglow with forty shades of delicate spring green. The fragrance of thousands of opening tree buds perfumes the air. The earth is warming and the musty pungence of leaf mold drifts upward at every step. A hermit thrush offers an impromptu concert in a thicket by the parking lot.

"We live such a rich existence in this Superior Peninsula," I muse aloud. The peaceful moment is shattered as a silver SUV careens into the parking area and screeches to a halt. Two women adorned in brightly-colored fleece jackets emerge from the vehicle and hurry up to me. Without any preamble, the driver (I learn later her name is Doris) pulls a rectangular object from her pocket and punches several buttons in rapid succession.

Holding the yellow-rimmed display screen up close to my face, she announces triumphantly, "We are right here!"

Alas, I come unglued. Repressing an impulse to grab the GPS and toss it in the lake, I launch into a rant: "No!" I shout, "We are not 'right there' on the GPS, we are right here."

Somewhat forcefully, I herd the two women down to the shoreline.

"Look, listen, smell," I command. "See the mist rising near Ewing Point; smell the woods coming to life; listen to that thrush sing his wondrous melody. Be here, in this real place, not on the map."

As the rest of the hikers arrive, my rant winds down. Doris and her friend Elaine (and the new GPS), edge away from the agitated group leader. Now I am chagrined by my uncharacteristic out-of-control behavior.

Even as I greet the other participants and suggest we all leave our cares at the trailhead before sauntering into the beautiful spring morning, I am still brooding about the GPS incident.

Why, I wonder, do we impose technological devices between ourselves and the natural world? We are already well on the way to being separated from the earth by brick and concrete—and now there is a relentless march of electronic wizardry substituting for reality. Am I just getting old and crotchety?

To be sure, a Global Positioning Device is a useful tool. My two wilderness and fire management daughters always carry a GPS when they roam the wilderness of Montana and Oregon performing their duties. I am comforted to know that they possess such a device. However, it seems to me that most recreational explorers use the GPS as a novel toy.

In my opinion, for what pennies it is worth, our culture is very close to worshiping all the latest electronic gadgets: cell phones, I-pods, Blackberries, now I-pads . . . the list goes on. There are now so many ways of transmitting messages—while driving, walking, shopping, dining, even while hiking in the woods—and nothing much of substance to say. Does all this communication lead to real progress or, as Susan Jacoby suggests in *The Age of Unreason*, does the relentless chatter assure that no one is ever alone with her thoughts?

A few steps into the forest and, as it always does, Alma Nature wraps her soothing arms around the leader and nine participants. It is the height of the annual migration and birds are everywhere.

Flights of warblers, tiny bits of yellow, red and orange, flit all about us feeding on blackflies and mosquitoes. Nashvilles, Canadas and redstarts seem to display their ephemeral charms just for us.

Wildflowers—trillium, trout lily, bloodroot—carpet the forest floor. We stand quietly in a copse of tall hemlocks, totally in the moment, eyes, ears, noses, even taste buds alert, savoring the rich sensations. There is no need for conversation, not even identifying flowers or ferns—that will come later. Now we are mesmerized by the May morning.

In a state of grace, we wander over to McKeever Cabin, a rustic log structure that the Forest Service rents to hikers, skiers and hunters for a nominal fee. We sit on the benches and each person shares what he or she has heard or seen. Then, as if on some cosmic cue, we are treated to a musical coda. Close beside the cabin, we hear it: the clear pensive song of a white-throated sparrow. "Old Sam Peabody, Peabody, Peabody," he seems to chant with a rising, slightly quavering whistle. The song is pure and clear, like a cup of icy well water or a breeze from Lake Superior.

I can tell that no one wants to leave, but we all have promises to keep; reluctantly, we retrace our steps to the parking area. Near where the path comes close to the lake, a loon calls. We stop and try to spot the bird and it calls again, a more urgent tremolo.

Then one of the hikers pulls out a cell phone, quickly dials a number and says, "Listen to this, Julia," while extending the phone toward the calling loon. Apparently Doris sees something foreboding in my body language and moves close to where I am standing.

She speaks softly: "Forgive him, leader Emerick, for he knows not what he is doing."

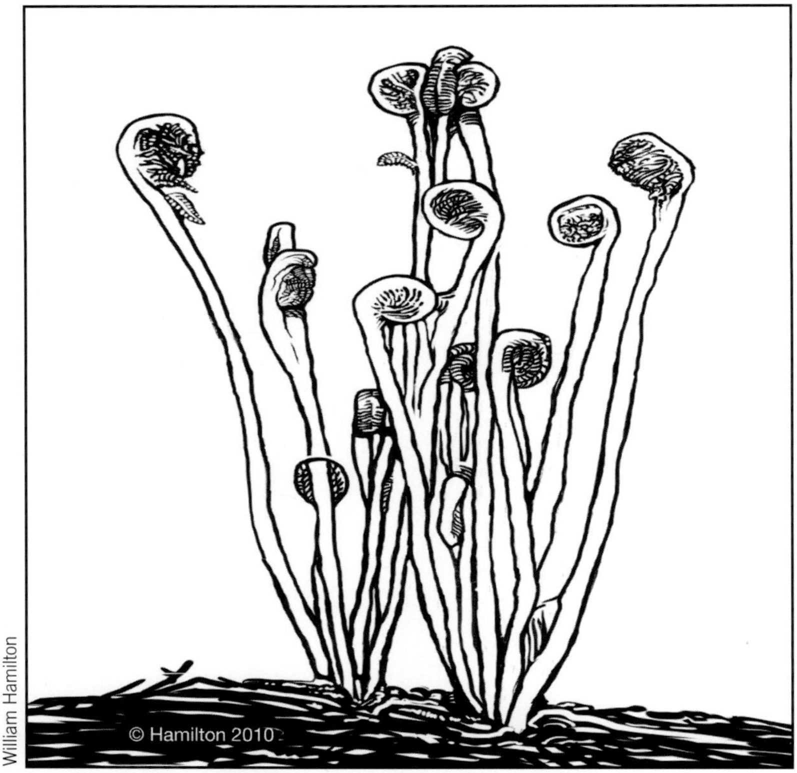
© Hamilton 2010
William Hamilton

THE PONDS

The trail spiraled down from a ridge of mature hardwood trees and entered a dense grove of mixed hemlock and white pine. We were in a state of grace after strolling through lush arrays of early spring wildflowers—hepatica, adder's tongue, Dutchman's breeches and spring beauty. Beside the path, we came upon a wooden Forest Service sign: The Ponds.

And there they were, on both sides of the trail, small ponds glistening in the sun. With a surge of excitement, we notice a convention of turtles on fallen logs along the edge of the water. Small turtles, large turtles, at least thirty-two of them by a rapid count. They seem to be enjoying a leisurely sunbath after the long winter.

We can't guarantee you will witness a gathering of turtles at The Ponds, but you will gather good memories. An undeveloped site in the Hiawatha National Forest (with only a very small, mostly hidden, back-country campsite), The Ponds is one of our favorite places simply to sit, quiet the noise and hurry of everyday life and revel in the natural sights and sounds. And it's possible you may experience a once-in-a-lifetime event in nature.

Several years ago, we took a small class of beginning birders to The Ponds in early May. As we approached the spot on the trail where you can see both ponds, a male scarlet tanager alighted on a branch just over our heads. The new birders let out an audible gasp as slanting rays of the morning sun lit up the bird's brilliant red plumage. Then, in a remarkable coincidence, a male Blackburnian warbler—so gaudily colored his nickname is Fire-Throat—landed in the same tree. Later, the students insisted we had prearranged this extraordinary event. We just smiled, knowing they had become enthusiastic new birdwatchers that day.

One year, we also celebrated Thoreau's birth date (July 12) at this remote site. All of us shared favorite passages from Walden and enjoyed the flute music provided by one member of the party. A flute player himself, Henry would have approved.

We owe a debt of gratitude to several prominent figures who had a vision for a national forest in the early 1900s. Theodore Roosevelt and Gifford Pinchot looked at a vast section of land—cut over and repeatedly burned—and pictured a verdant Hiawatha National Forest. They had to fight the powerful lumber barons who saw only board feet and more wealth. Fortunately, T.R. and Pinchot prevailed. In February 1909, Roosevelt set aside a huge reserve of land in the eastern part of the U.P. Almost exactly twenty-two years later, on February 12, 1931, Herbert Hoover added thousands more acres in the central Upper Peninsula.

We are now blessed with the Hiawatha National Forest: 879,000 acres, 400 lakes, miles of wild and scenic waterways, including such storied rivers as the Indian, Sturgeon, Whitefish and Stutts. More recent additions include Grand Island National Recreation Area, a jewel in Munising Bay, cabins in two locations that visitors can rent for a rustic stay, and wilderness areas closed to travel by all except foot and small water craft.

If it had not been for a few strong political leaders, The Ponds would have had a McMansion—or at least a covey of cottages—on the shorelines and be decorated with No Trespassing signs.

The best time for seeing wildflowers and birds near The Ponds is the second week in May; this may vary from year to year. The easiest way to get to The Ponds is to travel on M-94 (east from Marquette, west from Munising.) Right across M-94 from the Valley Spur Ski and Bike recreation site, look for Forest Service Road 2276. Proceed on this gravel road for about 1.3 miles, and watch for the blue-and-white North Country Trail markers on both sides of the road. Park on the right side at a wider part of the road, and follow the blue blazes on the left side of the road about a quarter-mile to The Ponds.*

If you continue north on FS 2276, you will come to pretty Coles Pond beside the road. It is named for Frank Cole, who had a camp here in the early 1900s.

Our own favorite way to get to The Ponds is a longer three-mile—but wonderful—walk on the North Country Trail. On M-94, look for Forest Service Road 2274 (also called AuTrain Camp Road because it was the site of a CCC camp). Proceed north on this gravel road about three miles until again you see North Country Trail markers. On your left is an open area for parking; the old CCC site with some remaining foundations is a short walk west on a grassy two-track road. After you check out the CCC site, return to the parking area, cross the road and head east toward The Ponds on the blue-marked trail. This trail section traverses hills and valleys, beautiful stands of beech and black cherry trees, with wildflowers covering every hillside.

A gentle reminder: "May no one say to your shame, All was beauty here until you came." Leave no trace of your passing, and give quiet thanks to the North Country Trail volunteers who maintain this pathway across the Upper Peninsula for us all.

* For a map of the Hiawatha National Forest, stop in the Visitor Center in Munising or contact Munising Ranger District, 400 E. Munising Avenue, Munising, MI 49862

HISTORIC HAYWIRE HIKE

When: Thursday, May 16

What: Hike a part of the route of the Manistique and Lake Superior Railroad (known as the "Haywire") which operated for logging and passenger service between Manistique and Shingleton starting in the late 1890s.

Trail: Level route on a former railroad grade. Possibly *WET* since it crosses 11 bridges and traverses wetlands. Borders the Big Island Wilderness at the southern portion. Excellent birding!

*H*aywire—bankrupt, "belly-up." Nickname for the Manistique & Lake Superior Railroad. A term applied to any outfit operating "on a shoestring" and "held together with baling wire." * Baled hay bound with thin wire was carried by the railroad for the logging camp horses. "Engineers used pieces of discarded haywire to make emergency repairs—enough to get back to the roundhouse and shops in Manistique." **

At the start of a hike on the old M&LS railroad bed, our small group looked down the narrow corridor stretching out before us. In our imagination, we could hear the train whistle and see the engine puffing slowly toward us near the end of its run from the lumbering town of Manistique.

Men bound for the lumber camps along the way, doctors and farriers making the camp rounds, schoolteachers going home for the weekend, hay for lumber camp horses, supplies and staples of all kinds were carried by railroads in the white pine boom days.

In *Lumberjack – Inside an Era,* Will Crowe writes of the time he and an employee of the Consolidated Lumber Company (successor to the Chicago Lumber Company) rode the "Haywire" from Manistique through Steuben, ending at Shingleton, then snowshoed seven miles in deep snow to check on a cedar cutting camp on the Upper West Branch of the Manistique River.

Steuben was a lively community around the turn of the last century, with a general store, hotel with restaurant and several logging camps in the surrounding woods. It was a center for logging drives down the Indian River to the mills in Manistique. Families often rode the "Haywire" train up from Manistique to have Sunday dinner at George Hughson's hotel in Steuben. Mrs. Hughson had a reputation for the best food around, and it was all-you-can-eat for fifty cents.

The M&LS railroad did indeed go bankrupt in 1920; other trains ran on the rails until 1968. Now, the thirty-three miles of abandoned right-of-way are part of the Hiawatha National Forest, and open to hikers, fisherpersons, hunters, snowmobilers and ATV riders. Today we would hike the eleven miles from Shingleton to Steuben.

Not far into our trek, we started to find small spikes left over from the pinning of the railroad ties—a blacksmith later told us the smallest spikes were the oldest. We took only a few, to be made later into candle holders, plant hangers and towel hooks.

The railroad bed was built through sandy plains and, in the northern sections, an extensive wetland. Soon after we left the northern trail head, just south of Shingleton, we came to the first of eleven bridge crossings on our route—including three branches of Stutts Creek. The anglers among us leaned into the shadows of the bridges, imagining the brook trout hiding there.

With each mile we hiked, the railroad corridor changed. We passed dry hummocks with huge white pine stumps that made good windbreaks for a lunch stop, then the ghost site of Scotts, founded in 1910 as a station on the railroad line. Finally, a sunny, sandy stroll along the edge of the Big Island Wilderness Area, with its myriad of small lakes, camping spots and canoe routes.

HAYWIRE TRAIL HIKERS

Lynn Emerick

When we came to Steuben in mid-afternoon, we hiked on just south of town to the railroad crossing of the Big Indian River. If we listened hard enough, it seemed we could hear the lumberjack shout of "timmmberrr" as the pines came down and could glimpse the river drive passing—part of our U.P. history that is not so very distant.

It had been a lovely day immersed in wild lands and history. Although we looked longingly south where the former rail corridor ran on out of sight and wondered what we might find around the next bend, that hike on the "Haywire" would have to wait for another day.

On the way home everyone was in a state of bliss, and afterglow of a wondrous experience into nature and our cultural heritage. I got to thinking how my life has been enriched in the company of white pines, the signature tree in our northern paradise.

Some trees are so distinctive in shape that even observers with no knowledge of forestry can identify them. Look on the horizon and there, rising above the other trees, are graceful plume-like branches extending horizontally and then angling upward toward the sky.

Pinus strobus. Eastern white pine, Michigan's State tree. The largest conifer growing in the eastern part of North America, the white pine has had a long and sometimes uneasy interaction with civilization.

SIGNATURE TREE OF THE U.P.

Did the immense stands of this beautiful tree have to be cut so rapidly and extensively? Fortune after fortune was made in the northern forests and the local residents were left with unemployment, ravished land and extensive wildfires. Those who preached caution, protecting some of the wild land and a slower approach at that time were derided as "google-eyed dudes, absent-minded professors and bugologists." (See *The Big Burn* by Timothy Egan.

Today in the Upper Peninsula we have only fragments of the vast stands of white pine that once graced this land. By exploring these remnants for more than four decades, I've learned many lessons from these magnificent trees.

What I learned from white pines

1. Stand tall and stalwart, but bend with the wind
2. Reach for the light
3. Exalt life with upraised arms
4. Make music in your own style
5. Endure the trials of life, and persevere
6. Be a harbor of refuge for wildlife
7. Cultivate patience
8. Get rid of deadwood that weighs you down

9. Be open to all possibilities but wear a protective skin

10. When you fall, continue to pay it forward as a nursery for the next generation

*Definition of Haywire from: *Lumberjack: Inside an Era in the Upper Peninsula of Michigan,* by Wm. S. Crowe. 50th Anniversary Edition edited by Lynn McGlothlin Emerick and Ann McGlothlin Weller 2002.

** Additional definition of Haywire from *Lumberjacks and Other Stories* by Jack Orr, 1983.

DANCING CRANES

It is an unexpectedly mild evening in early April and a fine time to look for the first signs of spring. There is an ecstasy among dwellers in this northern climate, a delight in every small portent that the vernal season of green, wild flowers and moving water soon will arrive.

After the long winter, the hunger is on us: We will mosey along Beckman Road in West Branch Township to savor the arrival of spring. Parking the car near the bridge over the Chocolay River, we marvel at the surging water. There, look, a small gray bird wagging his tail and calling his name, "Phoebe." He seems to be inspecting the underside of the bridge for a nesting spot.

Although snow lingers in the woods, the old farm fields lie open and the aroma of the rich soil emerging from lengthy hibernation is in the air.

Moving slowly, we approach an abandoned farmhouse surrounded by huge fields. There, not more than thirty yards away, is a pair of Sandhill Cranes performing their courtship ritual.

The huge birds face each other, bob their heads up and down in a bowing motion, then leap upward with their feet thrust forward. Landing in an almost-ballet movement, the birds compose themselves, leap again, and repeat the entire sequence several times.

Sandhill Cranes are imposing birds—four feet tall, with a seven-foot wingspan. They sport a red crown, a soft-gray body, long dark legs and a clump of tail feathers that resemble an old-fashioned bustle.

SANDHILL CRANE

In the first half of the twentieth century, the population of Sandhill Cranes was dangerously low due to liberal hunting seasons and the destruction of wetland habitat. Now the birds are making a comeback, both locally and across parts of the nation.

The courting cranes must have sensed they were being watched. Suddenly they took flight, called in unison (experts try to use words to portray the call—"gahr-o-o-o-oo" often is used, but you have to hear it for yourself), circled the field and headed toward the east.

When I took an early retirement from Northern Michigan University, my goal was to spend the last chapters of my life connecting people with nature. I intended to accomplish this through my writing and by sharing my lifelong interest in birds.

Over and over again I have witnessed the surprise and enjoyment people derive from watching and learning about birds. Sometimes a single sighting, perhaps of a scarlet tanager glowing in the sunlight, is enough to transform a casual observer into a devoted birdwatcher. In order to promote these opportunities, I launched Schools of Birding. For a day, or even an entire weekend, participants immerse themselves in the world of birds. Using a simple mnemonic, the neophytes learn how to systematically observe and sort out identification cues: How *Big* is the bird; what salient *Markings* does it have; how does it *Act*; where does it *Live*; what *Colors* does it show; what *Song* does it have? *Big Mac And Large Chocolate Shake.* Corny, I know, but people remember it and it works!

The response has been very gratifying—scores of neophyte naturalists have been transformed into enthusiastic birdwatchers. Best of all, once they are exposed to this new colorful world in their own backyards, they become advocates. When they see an indigo bunting, hear the flute-like call of a hermit thrush or thrill to a flight of sandhill cranes, they want their children, grandchildren and at least the next seven generations to be able to have these same experiences.

If you would like to see Sandhill Cranes this spring in the central Upper Peninsula, look in open fields southeast of Marquette and many sites in Alger County. The Green Garden area south of Marquette, the fields north of Sundell and Rumely, and around the hamlet of Traunik are good spots for viewing cranes in April. Be sure to bring binoculars for close-up views. Always respect private property.

In September, resident Sandhill Cranes gather to make the annual fall migration. Large numbers of the birds can be seen in assembly sites west of the AuTrain Basin in Alger County. If you would like to see (and hear) thousands of cranes assembling, go to the Platte River in Nebraska in late March/early April. Kearney (Nebraska) is one town that caters to crane-watchers with festivals, other special events and even "crane-trains" for transport of visitors to watching sites!

ROADSIDE TREASURES

Michigan has one of the best, if not the best, system of roadside rest stops in the nation, When you travel about in the Upper Peninsula, note how scenic and appealing are the thirty-one rest stops (and many more scenic turnouts) which grace the highways of our Superior Peninsula. When you do, take the time to give thanks to K. I. Sawyer.

Kenneth Ingalls Sawyer (his mother's cousin was Laura Ingalls Wilder of the *Little House on the Prairie* fame) is perhaps best known as the man who created the safety innovation of painting white dividing lines on highways and for his later work siting airports. But it was also his idea to create roadside parks for motorists.

One noon, so the story goes, Sawyer was sitting on a rock eating his lunch along U.S. Highway 2 between Crystal Falls and Iron River when he got the idea of placing picnic tables at convenient spots for motorists. Larson Park is now the roadside rest stop closest to where Sawyer had his "ah-ha" moment.

We have stopped at almost all of these roadside parks in the U. P. While we have enjoyed respites at each site, we do have some favorites. Here, listed by region, are several of them (See also *Gentle Hikes of Upper Michigan*, by Tornabene, Volgelsang and Morgan).

Keweenaw Peninsula:

Esrey Park. There are so many scenic sites in the Copper Country, it is difficult to choose one. But Esrey Park, located on the rocky Lake Superior shoreline between Eagle Harbor and Copper Harbor on M-26, is a special favorite for us. More than fifty years ago, we spent many hours enjoying this park while on our wedding trip.

High rock shelves afford superb views of Lake Superior; at that time ore freighters navigated much closer to the shore, so close in fact that we could make out the names of the ships

We swam in chilly water, hunted for agates on the beach, strolled along the majestic shoreline and watched the sunset—it seemed to "sink" directly into the lake's silken surface.

Western Upper Peninsula:

Agate Falls. Located on M-26 between Trout Creek and Bruce Crossing, this wayside features large pines and, across the road, a walk to a beautiful waterfall. And let me say, not in an ascetic way, memorable goodies at a nearby gift shop, soon to be rebuilt.

Canyon Falls. There are very few canyons in the Upper Peninsula, certainly not on the scale of those found in Arizona, Utah and other western states. But here where the Sturgeon River flows through a narrow, steep-walled rock gorge, we have a canyon that is thrilling enough, it will serve. Plan to visit this lovely spot in all seasons; see the waterfalls in full roar in spring, sit on the rock ledges near the falls in summer and autumn. Winter is a great time to see spectacular ice formations in many hues as the river freezes in interesting shapes, patterns and colors; the trail along the top of the rock outcroppings also makes a great snowshoe hike. Canyon Falls park is located on U.S. 41 south of L'Anse.

Central Upper Peninsula:

Scott Falls. Highway M-28 runs very close to Lake Superior at several points between Marquette and Munising. If you haven't made a stop at Scott Falls Park, you've missed a wonderful spot for a respite. This roadside park offers everything, a waterfall and sandstone cave, a pleasant picnic area under tall pines, a pristine sand beach, a launching point for canoes and kayaks, a new board walk and an historic face carved in a sandstone ledge. (*The Face in the Rock* by Loren Graham).

Grand Island Harbor Overlook. On the western edge of Munising, atop an impressive hill, is a roadside park offering stunning views of Grand Island and vast stretches of the Pictured Rocks National Lakeshore. In late afternoon, it is very difficult to leave this wondrous place: the slanting rays of the sun light up the towering sandstone cliffs of colored stone, framed by the greatest of the Great Lakes.

Eastern Upper Peninsula:

Manistique River. One mile south of Germfask (stop and ask the locals how the village got its name) is a pleasant roadside park on the historic Manistique River. Like many of the peninsula's rivers, the Manistique served as a travel route and is now extensively used by recreational canoeists and kayakers. In the last decades of the 19th century, thousands of white pine logs were floated down the river to the sawmills in Manistique.

Plan also to visit the Seney National Wildlife Refuge in this area; it is located just north of Germfask on M-77. Established in 1935 as a haven for migratory birds, its 96,000 acres of forest, marsh, lakes and open grasslands draws common loons, bald eagles, osprey, a myriad of waterfowl including geese, ducks and nesting Trumpeter Swans. The staff and volunteers at the excellent visitor center are delighted to share their knowledge of this unique refuge.

DeTour Roadside Park, on M-177 just west of the village of Detour, is a delightfully shady roadside rest stop. The park is situated on the far northern shore of Lake Huron and offers picnic tables scattered under huge white cedars and excellent views of the Les Cheneaux archipelago.

Les Cheneaux, "The Channels," features thirty-six islands. The villages of Hessel and Cedarville are as close to a "water world" as you can find in the peninsula. Boats are everywhere; a boat building school passes along classic techniques to its students; there is an excellent maritime museum; among other events, an annual wooden boat show and festival of arts draws thousands to Cedarville on the second Saturday in August.

The Upper Peninsula roadside parks, in addition to offering scenic places of respite during travel, are also good places to look for birds—particularly those parks that are close to water. The last time we saw a redheaded woodpecker, a bird increasingly harder to find, was at Old Flowing Well Park, located six miles east of McMillan on M-28. Canyon Falls, DeTour and Manistique River Park are all good spots for seeing spring warblers.

To locate any of Michigan's roadside parks, check the interactive Michigan Department of Transportation map at www.mi.gov, using the Search Term: *Roadside Parks.*

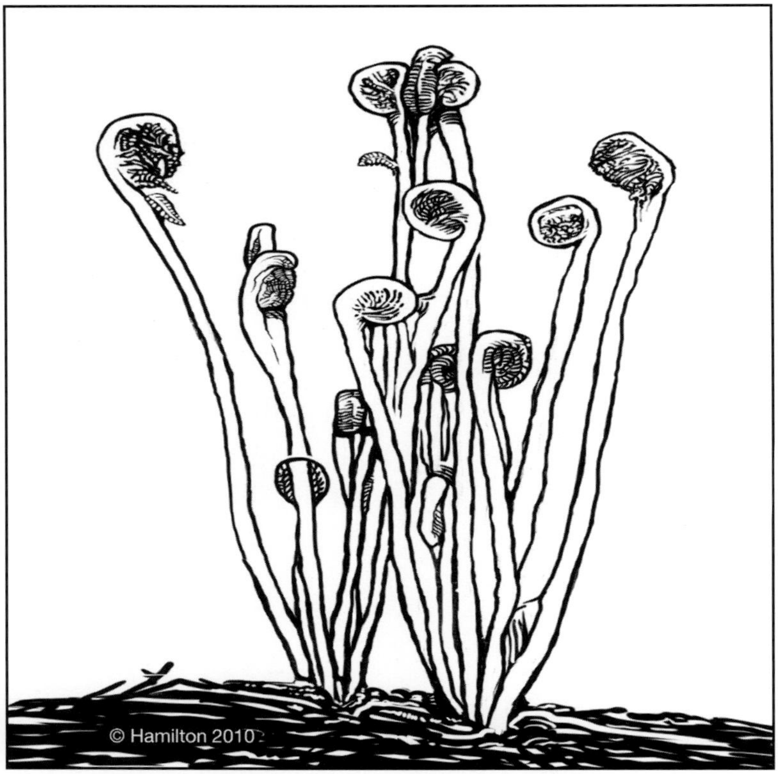

William Hamilton

THE FLAG PROJECT

It was time to plant the final flag. Reverently, with joy and hopefulness, we place the small green banner with large white letters proclaiming "Save the U.P." near the very tip of the Keweenaw Peninsula. The pennants were already waving at the other three corners of the Upper Peninsula—near Ironwood, Detour and Brimley. We had tramped in nature preserves, along Lake Superior beaches, by small lakes and under rugged cliffs. The Four Corners Mission was accomplished.

Symbolically, we are "claiming" the territory above the Big Mac Bridge for all the residents who love this rugged land and the lifestyle that is our privilege to enjoy. It also is an effort—quixotic, perhaps—to call out danger, to signal a warning about the epidemic of "development" defined, of course, as "progress" that is sweeping inexorably across this Superior Peninsula.

Images of "Up North" lure people—especially those jaded with urban living—to the U.P. Those who come with an appreciation of the land and its people have contributed much to their new communities.

Some newcomers, though, come with an idealistic view of this region, bringing expectations of transplanting an urban lifestyle into a remote and rugged place. There is a tendency to set out making this new place more like the places they have fled. In his book *Great Lakes Journey*, William Ashworth delineated the Fallacy of Composition: "Things you want add up to things you don't want."

Do you remember the parable of the frog?

> An eighth grade science teacher put a frog in a pot of water and asked the class to watch closely. Placing the glass container on a burner, he slowly turned up the heat. The frog floated happily as the water temperature warmed—it seemed to go into a sleepy torpor. As the temperature increased in slow increments, the frog continued to nap, never moving, never showing concern. Finally, as the water began to boil, the frog died as the astonished students watched. The teacher then selected a second

live frog and, ignoring the gasps of his students, plopped it into the boiling pot. The frog immediately jumped out. The moral, of course, is that numerous slow changes lull us into a sense of complacency until all those small changes add up to "what we don't want" for our home territory.

We are wary, too, when others come here who see only dollars in our natural heritage. One local land developer is marketing the U.P. to out-of-area buyers with the slogan, "Escape while you can!" Escape what? To what?

A short while after those ads appeared, a couple from Texas purchased a large tract of land on Lake Superior. Although they had some doubts about "global warming," they decided to hedge their bets by having a retreat in the far north, just in case. Some retreat. They built a nine-thousand square foot house with four bedrooms and four bathrooms. After settling in, they started to complain: the local shopping opportunities were limited; the road was gravel and not plowed promptly after a snowstorm; there was not enough variety of restaurants; the local residents were unfriendly and ignored the No Trespassing signs, and so forth. They may have "escaped" but brought it all with them to the U.P.

We remember that the human history of our peninsula has been one of boom and bust: resources are harvested as quickly as possible, with most profits siphoned off and sent away to other states and countries. And we are left with empty promises and unsightly or dangerous residue.

Living long in a place, one is bound to see changes in the land and destruction of favorite natural areas. Many of us who dwell in the Upper Peninsula cannot live happily without opportunities to savor beauty, the rapture of silence and wild spaces. We echo Thoreau's lament penned a century and a half ago: "I am attempting to read the 'Book of Nature' all the while others are rapidly tearing out the pages."

FOUR CORNERS MISSION AT PORCUPINE MOUNTAINS

What we have here in this peninsula is vulnerable to each new proposal to convert the land and its resources into corporate profit. We must be careful not to allow destruction of the very reasons we wish to live here.

Every day, longtime lovers of this Superior Peninsula offer thanks—each in his or her own way—that we are fortunate to live in this wild and beautiful land. With the flags planted on the four corners of the U.P., we make a small statement of affection and concern for our native valley.

If, by chance, you discover one of the small banners, please leave it in place and let us know the date and place of your discovery.

Photo: Mark Mitchell

Summer

Lon Emerick

Lon Emerick

Evan Premo

Mark Mitchell

72 SUMMER

Summer
INTRODUCTION

Residents of the Upper Peninsula often use humor to describe summers in the far north. Be advised that we make these jokes to alarm tourists and prospective immigrants to our part of paradise. Here are some examples of responses to our chilly summers:

"I hope summer this year is on the 4th of July."

"Three weeks of poor skiing, time to thaw out a bit, take our annual bath, entertain hordes of bugs and visitors—and get ready for winter."

A nurse from a local emergency room insists: "We've seen several cases of hypothermia here in the local hospital during blueberry picking season. In August!"

These anecdotes are all true, even the two I made up.

All kidding aside, Yoopers do get a bit out of control when it warms up. No more swamper boots, mittens, heavy wool coats, snow scoops, roof rakes, pipes to thaw. Finally, freedom from cabin fever.

No one wants to go anywhere during our short summer—there is so much to see and do here: long distance hiking, exploring old woods roads, going to camp, visiting favorite waterfalls. One favorite pastime is gathering summer's bounty of wild fruit: strawberries in June; raspberries in July; blueberries in August. Come on along as we journey into a U.P. summer.

William Hamilton

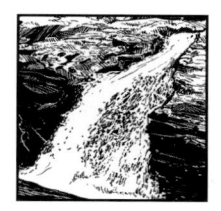

COOL, CLEAR WATER

Water: cool, clear water. How elemental it is to our lives, to all life. We humans are fascinated with lakes and rivers; watching waves and riffles evokes ancient memories and stirs deep and pleasant emotional images. In his hauntingly lyrical book *The Immense Journey*, anthropologist Loren Eisley writes that "if there is any magic on the planet, it is contained in water."

Water is indeed magical. Water—the same water over and over—circulates constantly between earth and sky. Each day, millions of gallons of the precious liquid evaporate into the atmosphere, condense into clouds and then fall back to the earth as rain or snow. Since our lives, to say nothing of the planet's, depend upon water, it is sobering to remember that our supply is limited to what we presently have—no more is being made.

Rarely are we out of sight of rivers—ever moving, winding and free, splashing and cascading over rocky cornices. There are more than 140 waterfalls in the Upper Peninsula ranging from small leaps to the thundering Tahquamenon.

Most of us are enchanted by waterfalls—the sounds, the sight and the feeling of power bombard all our senses. The water speaks to our spirit and the message is soothing. Many people find a reduction of stress and discomfort sitting beside one of the peninsula's waterfalls. Thoreau knew of this long ago when he wrote about the tonic of wild places.

We revel in the sound of moving water, and when the opportunity arose to purchase Pinnacle Falls on the pristine Yellow Dog River in northern Marquette County, local residents came through once again. Lovers of the Yellow Dog River Watershed raised a large sum of money; now the spectacular falls and the surrounding land is open for all to visit and receive its glad tidings.

Cool, clear water running free for you and me.

Sadly, however, there are powerful forces stalking the Yellow Dog plains and they are willing to sacrifice a wild river in an effort to extract minerals under the Salmon Trout River, which flows into the Yellow Dog, then into Lake Independence and the Iron River, and finally into Lake Superior. If toxic drainage from a mine in sulfide ore on the Yellow Dog plains leaks into the water of the Salmon Trout River (or any of the other myriad streams and water courses in the area), it will eventually reach Lake Superior. This largest of the Great Lakes accounts for fully 10% of the planet's fresh water. Yes, the planet is composed mostly of water, but only about 2 ½ percent of that is drinkable. Clean water is fast becoming more precious than gold or oil.

The Kennecott Minerals Corporation, subsidiary of the foreign-owned Rio Tinto Company, is moving ever closer to mining copper and nickel on the plains and under the river. The problem is that the ore—with an estimated value of two billion dollars—is embedded in sulfide rock. When sulfide ore is mined and exposed to air and water, the combination can produce the powerful chemical sulfuric acid, the same chemical used in auto batteries.

A sulfide mine carved out under the Salmon Trout River? Why not build a garbage incinerator at Jefferson's Monticello, convert the Grand Canyon into a landfill or drill for oil under the Mormon Tabernacle in Salt Lake City?

Yes, I acknowledge the need for metals in our modern economy. My own Cornish ancestors chipped out a future for me in the copper mines of the Keweenaw Peninsula. But all mines are not created equal. The proposed mine in sulfide ores on the Yellow Dog plains would not be my grandfather's mine.

The type of mine that Kennecott is planning has *never been accomplished without the release of toxic substances on contact with air and water*. We are told by the company that each such documented accident at their other mines was "human error" or a "weather event." As far as we know, there will be humans operating a planned mine and weather events, including snow and rain storms, are a common occurrence on the water-rich Yellow Dog plains. What other way can we judge future performance than by prior efforts?

The company promises to be careful and even with glaring gaps in their ever-changing permit applications, asks that we trust them. It's tempting. Then we wouldn't have to deal with a vexing issue any more. But then I remember other promises:

> "DDT is safe." (And spring came and no birds sang; we all carry DDT in our bodies.)

> "Reserve Mining is environmentally responsible." (Tons of what were called benign tailings were dumped from the Reserve mine site north of Duluth into Lake Superior—then asbestos-like fibers showed up in Marquette's harbors near drinking water intakes.)

> *"Cigarettes are not harmful." (Tell that to the families of millions of lung cancer victims.)*

Who will control the future of this land? The people who live in the Upper Peninsula or officers of a corporation based in a remote country? The mining companies will pocket most of the revenues and, as so many times and so many companies in the past, will leave the residents with a toxic legacy in their back yard.

It has been disconcerting to observe the actions and decisions of the Michigan Department of Environmental Quality during the lengthy permitting process for the proposed mine. It seemed to some that the DEQ was focused on assisting Kennecott Minerals rather than carrying out their mission to protect the environment. It appeared from the outside that the agency was more focused on the prospect of economic development than rigorous scrutiny of the company's record in past and current mining operations. The contrast with what happened after completion of mining at a comparable Kennecott site in Wisconsin is striking. Now, by law, any future applications for mining permits in Wisconsin must demonstrate a successful history pollution-free operations during and for years after mining operations. No company has been able to provide such a history and no further permits for mining in sulfide ore have been issued in that state.

Kennecott Minerals is proposing the building of a new 22-mile roadway through the Michigamme Highlands, crossing 24 rivers or creeks, installing 79 culverts, impacting 27 acres of wetlands and building six new concrete bridges to bring the ore to a mill in Humboldt for crushing and processing. Imagine the potential of sulfide contamination with 100 trucks per day traversing this (formerly) wild land.

The Keweenaw Bay Indian community considers Eagle Rock, a large stone outcropping on the plains, to be a sacred site. They have objected to Kennecott's intent to blast the rock to create a mine shaft around and under the stone. The Natives gather to pray at this site. After a judge advised that Eagle Rock be preserved as a Native American worship site and suggested that another mine shaft entrance could be found nearby, the company responded that Eagle Rock was their best and least expensive site for the shaft. The DEQ then decided that a site cannot be a religious place unless it is a building!

Paraphrasing Barry Goldwater's famous speech to the Republican party: *Extremism in the love of the land is no vice; moderation in the pursuit of environmental goals is no virtue.*

To mine or not to mine—that is the question. To me, sulfide mining involves unacceptable risks to water, air, land and way of life in this superior peninsula. The risks will be ours—and our rewards will be very few.

> *"The beauty of the living world . . . has always been uppermost in my mind . . . I have felt bound by a solemn obligation to do what*

I could—if I didn't at least try I could never be happy in nature . . . there would be no peace for me if I kept silent."

–Rachel Carson (1907-1964)

KEWEENAW MAGIC

At least once a year, usually more often, I am compelled to visit the land of my Cornish ancestors. Often it coincides with the Copper Harbor Festival which features the music of *White Water,* the Premo family band from Amasa.

I find myself drawn to the Copper Country not only because my roots are there, but also because of the surcease I feel when I contemplate its rugged charm. When scenery was handed out, the Keweenaw Peninsula must have been at the head of the line. Its shoreline, particularly the stretch between Eagle River and Copper Harbor, is incomparable; in the same area are the starkly beautiful Brockway Mountains; throughout the peninsula, rivers—the Montreal, Gratiot, Silver—surge down narrow gorges, tumbling and foaming toward Lake Superior.

Located at the tip of the peninsula is the Estivant Pines, a tract of huge virgin white pines; one leaning giant measured seven feet in diameter. Dotting the region are tranquil granite-ringed inland lakes—Medora, Lac La Belle, Gratiot and others. Dominating the landscape are trees—maples, oaks, birches and rank upon rank of pines.

There is also ample evidence of the courage and persistence of the early pioneers—rusted old headframes, long-closed mine shafts, piles of dark waste rock and ghost towns. Lonely, silent and crumbling, they bear only a shadowy resemblance to their former lively existence.

At the end of another delightful weekend of music and exploring the Keweenaw Peninsula, Dean and Bette Premo asked us for a favor. Of course—we agreed without knowing what we would be asked to do.

It started out as a simple task: We were to transport composer/musician Jukka Linkola and his wife Marita from Copper Harbor, where they had been attending the annual art and music festival, to our home in West Branch Township. Linkola was in the U.P. for the premiere of his Bass Concerto during Finn Fest 2005. The Linkolas were scheduled on a night flight back to Finland. Since we live close to Sawyer Airport, we could provide them a place to rest and have supper before the long journey to Helsinki. Little did we know we were to have an epic adventure and the seamless union of three European cultures that had a profound impact on the settlement of the Upper Peninsula.

Even though there was a language barrier—Jukka speaks accented English and we know no Finnish—it was a pleasure to share time with these talented people. Jukka and Marita were interested in the Keweenaw Peninsula and were surprised to see so many roads and mailboxes with Finnish names. "Korpi," "Niemi," "Maki," they exclaimed as we drove along US-41.

As we approached the ghost town of Central Mine, I asked if they would like to see where my Cornish ancestors lived when they immigrated to the U.P. in 1860. They would like that very much.

After stopping at the new visitor center, we decided to show them the distinctive old Methodist Church. Although the church is only open to the public for the annual reunion of Cornish descendants in late July, a volunteer was busy painting the building exterior. Fortuitously, his name was Penrose, a common Cornish name, and I (a Trezona and Chewidden by ancestry) used my Celtic charm and common heritage to get us a look into the church.

Jukka was transfixed by the stark simplicity of the interior and explored eagerly. Then he spied the harmonium, donated to the church by Sacred Heart Parish of Laurium. Sitting down at the keyboard, he opened a hymnal and soon a wonderful melody enveloped all of us. I sat in a back row pew, thinking I might be in the exact spot where my great-great-grandfather, Samuel Satterly, listened to the very same hymn in 1870.

Hearing the sound of the lovely old harmonium, Mr. Penrose entered the church and was stunned. He swayed to the music and closed his eyes in delight. Later, when Jukka had finished the hymn, he and Penrose chatted and exchanged e-mail addresses.

Glowing from the experience, I impulsively stopped at Slim's Café in Mohawk and purchased a bag of Scottish scones. Immigrants from Scotland also enriched the Upper Peninsula. As we happily sampled the scones, Lynn described her Scots-Irish grandfather's experiences during the U.P.'s white pine lumbering era in the late 1800s and early 1900s.

Although the afternoon was waning, we knew the Linkolas would want to see the historic Hanka Homestead north of Baraga, now a participating site with the Keweenaw National Historic Park. We arrived at the site just as the docent was preparing to leave. When we introduced Jukka to Reuben Niemisto and told him the reason the Linkolas were in the U.P., the two men held an excited conversation in Finnish. The only word we recognized was "poika" which means "boy" or "son." It seems that Mr. Niemisto's son Paul had recommended Jukka for the commission of the Finn Fest concerto composition.

A blending of Cornish, Scottish and Finnish—we were overwhelmed at the synchronicity of our afternoon. The only sound in the car for the rest of the trip was munching on scones as we all meditated about the wonders that had occurred.

The chorus from Craig Johnson's poignant song, *"Keweenaw Lights"* ran through my mind all the way home.

> *"The stars shine bright on the south shore tonight,*
> *And the Keweenaw Light sweeps over the Bay.*
> *And if dreams could come true, I'd still be there with you,*
> *On the banks of cold water at the close of the day."*

One of the joys of living here is that our heritage is close at hand—the history is still alive and dwells in us.

William Hamilton

GOIN' CAMP

Words, words, words. It is Friday afternoon and the weekly faculty meeting grinds on at a glacial pace. "Minutes are kept and hours are wasted," I muse as the departmental chairman drones on and on about the library budget. Then I escape mentally, as I always do, out a nearby window. A white-throated sparrow is singing in a juniper bush and he seems to proclaim: "Time to go to camp, camp, camp."

June is summoning and I must respond to her siren call. The truck is packed and backed into my parking slot for a rapid exit—as soon as this painful academic process is finished. I shall abandon everything and go to my camp, the AuTrain Hermitage.

Going to camp: How sweet the sound of that phrase. The expression certainly is unique to the Upper Peninsula. Here we call all woodland dwellings—anything from a simple hunting shack to an elaborate log lodge—"camps." Rarely do you hear residents announce they are going to their cottage or summer home. Nope, we "go to camp," an expression sometimes compressed into a declaration, "Goin' camp."

There are hundreds of camps scattered throughout this magnificent country and each has a special history. The story of a camp is a saga of the people. Who built it and why? Has it had one or several owners throughout the years? How many generations have crossed this threshold, slept in these bunks? And so much more. But in each instance, there are certain universal feelings we all have about our forest sanctuary. When we transfer from town to camp, from work-a-day world to time of leisure, in a very real sense we assume another life.

Even though the hunger for camp is on me, I savor the familiar drive—the journey is an important element in the transition. Inspecting the roadsides for any changes since my last visit, I admire the unfolding array of wildflowers as summer progresses, marvel at how the ravens wheel and soar in a cobalt sky, and watch closely for wildlife crossing the highway. The closer I get to camp, the more my anticipation quickens.

Sometimes I stop and spend a few minutes with my friend Stanley, who resides on the gravel road leading to the Hermitage. A vigorous octogenarian and master gardener, Stanley has a way of helping me sluff off the last remnants of intellectual baggage and Type A behavior lingering in my psyche. I think he can read my metabolism. One day not too long ago, I arrived at Stanley's door all harried and worn. He took one look at me and observed, "So, too many books again. Here," he commanded, handing me a hoe. "Go and hoe the beans for a while and when you're slowed down, we'll have some of Myrtle's raisin pie." I am always better prepared for camp when I leave Stanley's house.

Finally, I make the last sharp turn on the narrow forest road and behold the cedar cabin waiting in a small clearing beside the Superior Lake.

I am always exhilarated by the immensity of the ice water mansions; the lake stretches out to the horizon, all the way to Canada, almost 160 miles north. Here is my ecological address; the aura of this gorgeous body of water has seeped into my DNA.

No question about it, Lake Superior is a dominant force in this region. It is like a good and constant companion—cold, aloof and capricious, to be sure—and a source of inspiration. We feel the lake's influence on our thoughts, our moods, our entire lives. Its presence is commanding.

All the superlatives about Lake Superior are true. It is the largest, coldest, deepest and roughest of the Great Lakes. As I admire the lake shimmering in the sun, it is hard to believe this robust body of water is so fragile.

The lake is subject to several assaults: invasive species, diversions of water, toxins from industrial operations near its shores, and persistent organic pollutants. Investigation of water quality shows dangerous quantities of aldrin, DDT, toxaphene, PCBs, and dioxin, to name just a few.

Many people, particularly those who derive profit from the water source, but often those who simply don't want to be bothered by environmental issues—cite the old dictum, "The solution to pollution is dilution." On the other hand—there is no other hand! There can be no compromise when it comes to protecting Lake Superior, which has 10% of the world's fresh water supply. (See *Cold, Clear and Deadly* by Melvin Visser).

For all those who love Lake Superior, the pivotal question is this: Is any economic gain worth the price we would pay in the decline of its water quality? Can we endorse any development which results in the warning that children and women of childbearing age should not consume fish taken from what was once the purest lake? Can we agree to *any* action, such as siphoning off water for sale to parched regions, which may have dire consequences for the ecological balance of the Peninsula's entire watershed?

The peevish cry of a gull who wants to rest on the sandstone spit jutting out into the lake rouses me from my reverie. I must arise now and repair to the log cabin, regain some serenity, and be ready to resist the forces poised to affect this great lake.

For some, opening camp requires an elaborate checklist and hours of labor. I simply open the door and kick out the mice and spiders. Yet opening the door, particularly after a long absence, is a spiritual moment. In his hauntingly lyrical book, *The Clam Lake Papers,* Edward Lueders describes how I, too, feel when I enter the AuTrain Hermitage.

> *"As I removed the storm door and turned the key in the lock of the inner door, I felt the quiet enchantment that I re-experience each summer when I enter those precincts of my self that have lain inviolate through the deep winter awaiting my returning step, breath and touch."*

When I push open the dark curtains, light fills the rustic cabin—it also floods my heart. It is this other self we celebrate and nurture at camp. For most of us, going to camp represents an opportunity to unwind, shed the cares of everyday life, get away from it all. Sometimes it takes a while to shift our focus and get in tune with the slower rhythms of nature. Each of us in his or her own way rediscovers what Henry David Thoreau meant when he wrote about the importance of having a wide margin in one's life.

My favorite time at camp is the evening vespers. I like to sit on the open porch and watch the light fade and relish the quiet of eventide. It is then that the French voyageurs and native people can be heard above the sound of waves gently laving the rocky shore. It is then, in the magical gloamin', that I hear them beach their canoes and gather firewood to prepare supper. It is then that I wander down to make the visitors welcome and discover only a lone gull resting on the long sandstone spit.

In our modern hectic world, many of us experience deficit living, a form of existence whereby the daily demands exceed our physical and mental resources. At camp we recharge our batteries. We go not to rough it, but to smooth out the wrinkles of our other life.

Alas, there are some people who cannot, or will not, adapt to life at camp. I dread the arrival of some who bring their fast-paced restlessness with them. The pattern is numbingly familiar. At first they exclaim over the serenity of the Hermitage. They usually flop into the hammock, maybe even doze a bit. By evening, the reality hits them: There is no evening paper, they are missing Katie Couric, there is no phone to check for messages, there is no power to plug in the laptop. The quiet and serenity begin to pall. Cozy slips to confining and relaxation segues into tedium.

The most restless visitors make some excuse and hastily depart. But a few turn their nervous energy to the enthralling fun of overhauling the Hermitage. Usually they disguise their pointed advice thinly by asking rhetorical questions: "Don't you think that power (substitute any modern noun—a shower, a lawn, an updated water system) would be a good addition here?"

The most frequent and persistent question is this: "Why don't you cut down the line of trees in front of the cabin so you can see the lake?" They are never satisfied with my response: "I don't want the lake and the people on it to see me or the cabin." It is more satisfying to leave the shoreline as it was when the Ojibwa canoed past. Besides, the path to my watching place on the shore is less than twenty yards. I can saunter down and savor the lake up close at any time.

I can ignore the unsolicited advice but when a guest turns his restlessness into relentless activity ("I like to keep busy")—sweeping the floor, washing windows, painting rocks, tidying up the woods—well, then I get a bit churlish. It's best to simply pack up and head for town where the restless guest can access his modem or go to the mall.

You don't need me to tell you that packing up and heading back to town is not nearly as much fun as getting ready to go to camp. It's best to keep at some distance when I am closing up the cabin. I get surly when I shut off the propane and lock the door. A writer, whose name I cannot recall, but who must have a similar temperament, said this about ending an outdoor adventure, "I have always had difficulty negotiating the emotional topography of transitions." You bet. But then I realize that it is the contrast with town life that makes going to camp so appealing. Rather than a substitute for the realm of work and school, it is a corrective. Let me put it another way: You seek a place where your spirit will flourish; in return it soothes, inspires and shapes your life in myriad ways.

I have watched the waves, listened to a hermit thrush and, most of all, I have been enriched (with Keats) in the simple worship of a day.

FROM LAKE TO SHINING LAKE

The idea arose out of an excess of affection: A plan to hike the narrow waist of the Upper Peninsula, from Rapid River on Lake Michigan all the way to Lake Superior at Munising. Lovers' enthusiasms typically run to excess and we felt the need to embrace—in a single summer season—this superior peninsula from lake to shining lake.

To accomplish our mission, a dozen Upper Peninsulaphiles would follow the Bay de Noc-Grand Island Trail, an historic pathway on lands mostly within the Hiawatha National Forest. The Noquet Indians traveled the trail regularly to spend summers on Grand Island in Lake Superior, and returned to Little Bay de Noc on Lake Michigan to winter further south. French voyageurs used the path to transport furs to Green Bay.

The Bay de Noc—Grand Island trail has two major access points: in the south, two miles north of Rapid River on CR-509 in Delta County; in the north near Ackerman Lake, off M-94 in Alger County. The route then follows a connector trail past small ponds and over ridges to join the blue-blazed path of the North Country Trail, winding through Valley Spur Ski/Bike Center and on to Lake Superior in Munising.

BAY DE NOC—GRAND ISLAND HIKE LOGO

Our dedicated dozen elected to saunter northward and end at Lake Superior. We planned to complete two segments (about eight to ten miles per section) each month from June to August. A baton, adorned with one gull feather (symbolizing water) and a raven feather (representing land) was dipped into Lake Michigan at the start of the walk and into Lake Superior when we finished.

Trail Magic is a term often used by hikers on the Appalachian and other long distance trails to describe the special, unexpected things that happen when out in the wild. There was magic for us along the Bay de Noc-Grand Island Trail.

BAY DE NOC—GRAND ISLAND TRAILHEAD

• The discovery that despite a few road crossings and some scattered camps there is an astonishing amount of wild country along the trail, due to its location within the National Forest.

• Several small brooks—Bill's, Ten Dollar, Haymeadow, Cherry—bubbling and shining in the morning sun.

• A bench appearing at just the right place for tired hikers to sit and look over long, lovely vistas of the Whitefish River Valley coming into summer green.

• Rarely visited lakes—Lower 18 Mile, Davie and 17 Mile—with no human development. Bettie and Lynn vowed to return to the wild raspberry patches we found near one of the lakes.

• A wild pond just off the trail, with a mosquito-clearing wind, which we found at 11:30 one morning. A perfect bug-free lunch spot. When one hiker looked at his watch and said, "It's not time for lunch yet," Rob said quietly, "We're on Trail Time out here," and lunch was on!

• Remnants of old logging camps and crumbling foundations where the CCC men lived and worked.

• A magnificent stand of old growth pine, which Helen immediately dubbed *The Magic Forest*. Weeks later, we realized that this name for the beautiful grove had been adopted by us all when a puzzled local resident came to us, map in hand, and said, "I've looked and looked and I can't find the Magic Forest anywhere on this map!"

• A happy uproar when the women, walking ahead along the trail, spied the forty-mile trail marker as we approached Ackerman Lake.

In mid-August, our stalwart group of happy hikers dipped the baton in Munising Bay and repaired to the nearby pavilion for a pizza celebration. Although a bit sad to reach the end of our quest, we also were proud and pleased with our summer saga. We had seen another part of the peninsula intimately and made it ours without disturbing it or changing it for the next person—perhaps you—to pass that way.

If hiking the entire length of the trail is not for you, walking short segments can give access to many historic and scenic treasures of the trail. (One tip from vivid experience: unless you are extremely fond of wood ticks, don't hike the southern segments in June.)

To find out more about the Bay de Noc-Grand Island trail, call or visit the Forest Service in Munising at 387-2512 or Rapid River/Manistique at 474-6442. Ask for a copy of a free recreational opportunity guide, with trail description and map.

From Lake to Shining Lake

Our rules were set before the trip,
bring lunch and snacks to dine.
In weather bad to go, but just
mosquitoes were to whine.

A staff was dipped in shining lake,
the venture's start to mark.
The doughty group of hikers bold
at trailhead then did hark.

The purpose of this trip was this:
We heard it straight from Lon -
to tread the woodland quietly
and then walk silent on.

This silence lasted fifty steps
T'was broke by ughs and icks!
You mean all day we must go through
the valley of the ticks?

A hundred million ticks were there
all waiting to go north-
to jump on calf or leg or back
from grass to sally forth.

*But when the ticks were seldom seen
the second time around,
We looked at trees and plants and birds
and toads that did abound.*

*We lose a mate in segment one.
To fail is not a sin.
Her struggle may be ours some day
When aging does us in.*

*In segment two, the sky grew grey -
Our raingear we did don.
With many miles to go that day
we then proceeded on.*

*We hikers didn't whine too much
to give us all our due -
when ten plus miles (promised)
became eleven plus two.*

*Our stops for lunch were welcomed rests -
they made our packs so light.
The food was not by Julia Child,
yet savored was each bite.*

*Nutritious was the fare we ate
But oft' was heard a sigh
for just a little decadence -
strawberry-rhubarb pie.*

*The points at which we start and stop
were chosen with great care.
'Twas great to hear that telling phrase
there is a toilet there.*

*Through beauties rife and minor pain
from lake to lake with Lon;
And always was our motto thus
"and we proceeded on."*

© R. Yuill

AN ELEGY FOR THE ELM

*I*t was a dark, dreary day and gray clouds hung low, threatening rain, as I approached an abrupt curve in the road south of Cornell in Delta County. Filling the highway before me, its lovely vase-like form thrust insistently toward the sky, was a mature American elm tree. So overcome was I by the ache of years long gone that I had to pull off the macadam and surrender to the memories which spilled into my consciousness. Until that moment I hadn't realized how much my life was intertwined with elms and how much I missed this beautiful tree.

SOLITARY ELM TREE

I have had a relationship with this most lovely of street trees for more than six decades. American elms were the most widely planted city tree all across the east, midwest and as far south as eastern Texas. The elm was a graceful addition to the landscape, it grew swiftly and was resistant to air pollution. A mature tree might soar to one hundred feet tall and be five feet in diameter at its base. People loved them. How could they have known that too much of a good thing would lead to disaster?

A large elm guarded the corner of our rural homestead at my childhood home north of Detroit. I liked to sit against its rough bark in the cool shade on hot summer days, listen to the cicadas sing and admire the patterns of light and dark the sun cast through the leaves and on to the grass. Later I was allowed to climb up into the tree's dense foliage and I marveled at the tough, glossy leaves with sawtooth edges.

I nailed a board on a broad branch where I could perch and survey my world. It was on that very perch that I first noticed up close and personal the great variety of birds that inhabited our area. One day as I sat there pretending to be a pirate looking out for rich merchant ships, a small orange, black and white bird landed on a branch beside me. It was astonishingly pretty. Later, after consulting a bird identification book, I learned it was an American Redstart, a species of warbler and a summer visitor to Northern climes. This experience initiated a lifelong passion for birds, a passion which I would later pursue at college.

Like old friends, stately American elms were there to greet me on the campus of Michigan State University when I entered as a freshman majoring in wildlife biology. I studied beneath them, searched for birds among the branches and sauntered through the downed leaves beside the Red Cedar River with my future wife.

But my most intimate association with elms occurred during three summers when I worked as a tree trimmer in Birmingham, a wealthy suburb of Detroit. There I climbed hundreds of trees, sawed off limbs and helped on a crew which removed old or damaged trees. It was during those summers that I first encountered the disease that would devastate the American elm. Only later did I learn that the cure we used, promoted at the time as a chemical miracle, would turn out to be far worse than the disease.

Like a deadly stowaway, the disease came into the United States riding on elm logs imported from Europe. The logs were infested with a fungus—later called Dutch elm disease—which kills a tree by blocking the water-conducting vessels under the bark. The disease is spread from tree to tree by a small beetle that carries the spores of the fungus on its body. When the beetle burrows into the bark, the fungus is rubbed off the insect, thus infecting the tree.

The fungus struck the American elm trees like a plague. By the mid-1980s, the disease had begun to race through the monoculture of city elms. The alarm went out and panicked foresters and city managers turned to a compound, dichloro-diphenyl-trichlororethane, which later became infamous as DDT. To control the disease, an extensive program of spraying designed to kill the beetles was launched.

In Birmingham, we sprayed continuously, always at night to avoid traffic and to ensure calm winds. The DDT was mixed with oil and sprayed in a mist so that it would cover the entire tree and stick to all the leaves and twigs. It took between two and five pounds of the mixture to cover a fifty-foot elm, and most of the trees on the streets were eighty feet, some even taller. The mixture stuck to everything: cars, street lights, children's toys; it dripped down on the grass, leaves and soil in the flower beds. The pesticide was safe, we were told, and we wore little or no protection. We did not know that we were doing a dangerous dance with an elixir of death.

In an attempt to allay concerns of the residents, the city manager arranged a meeting at a local school. All employees of the forestry division were required to attend. The manager assured the crowd that DDT and the city spraying program were totally safe. In a dramatic—if stupid—gesture, he spread a large dollop of DDT on a slice of bread and ate it!

During my first year of college, I discovered just how deadly DDT really was. Spring came to the Michigan State campus and no birds sang. Coincidentally, I was enrolled in an ornithology course taught by George Wallace, a renowned authority in the study of birds. Dr. Wallace was supervising a research investigation on robins when he and his assistant started finding dead and dying robins all over the campus. Postmortem examinations revealed very high concentrations of DDT in the birds' fat cells. What was happening?

Exploring further, Wallace found that DDT drifted down in the soil from the University's Dutch elm spraying program. Earthworms ingested the pesticide-laden soil and robins then ate the earthworms. The researchers showed that eating only eleven worms was a lethal dose for the unsuspecting birds. Ominously, it was discovered that DDT becomes even more concentrated as it travels up the food chain: large avian predators like bald eagles and peregrine falcons were rendered unable to reproduce and their numbers declined dramatically. Many observers asked: "What are we doing to the planet?"

George Wallace's robins, along with other research at the time, led to a monumental book, a volume that shocked the world into considering the consequences of the toxins being introduced into the environment. In many ways, *Silent Spring* by Rachel Carson, was the book which launched the modern environmental movement. Sadly, the wide use of DDT had done little to halt the spread of Dutch elm disease. So many trees were cut down that some city streets looked like a tornado had roared through town. The lovely American elm tree all but disappeared.

There may be reason for hope: the American elm is trying to make a comeback. Many experts in forestry science believe that it may happen naturally. They point out that the elm is an aggressive seeder and that scattered survivors might create a whole new generation of trees. Others are doubtful. The solution, they believe, may be genetic engineering. Researchers at Michigan State University are attempting to splice in genes from the Siberian elm, a tree that is resistant to Dutch elm disease. But, if successful, will the resulting tree be the American elm that we have come to know and love?

As you go about your appointed rounds, look for the few elms still holding on to life. They may be in your neighborhood, along the road to camp, or standing tall in an open field in the country. They are usually alone—solitary survivors of the elm disease holocaust; because they were loners, far away from others of their kind, the infecting beetles could not fly far enough to reach them.

Look along County Road 545 South in West Branch Township (after a sharp left curve, the elm tree is just to your right on the edge of a forest road); south of Trenary on U.S. 41 or just south of Cornell on County Road 420.

It will take a sharp eye, and perhaps a field guide, to find the young elms sprouting hopefully beside the roadway. Too small to host the elm beetle, they offer some encouragement to those of us who remember the American elm with fondness. May their magnificent graceful forms decorate the landscape in the next century.

A DAUGHTER OF THE LAND

She walks in beauty, like the night
Of cloudless climes and starry skies;
And all that is best of dark and bright
Meet in her aspect and her eyes . . . "
 —Lord Byron

The Upper Peninsula is home to many treasures—abundant clear waters, vast forests, cliffs of colored stone and so much more. Those who love this land are enriched by close contact with these natural treasures.

Human treasures also abound in these environs and enrich the lives of all who dwell on this pleasant peninsula. Often, when we celebrate our human treasures, we think of the peninsula's elders. Those who worked in the CCC camps, copper and iron mines, logging camps, who fought in foreign wars, taught the children, healed the sick, held down the home front. And they indeed are worthy of recognition and celebration, as we have tried to do in our books: *Lumberjack—Inside An Era* and *Going Back to Central (Mine)—On the Road in Search of the Past*.

Yet the Superior Peninsula also is rich in our youth who work and study here and do us proud, whether they stay or leave for more distant adventures.

One score and one year ago, a treasure was born in Iron County to the musically talented Premo family. Bette and Dean named her Laurel. Surrounded by music from her birth, Laurel joined the family band, *White Water* while still a wee lass, using a drummer's brush on a cardboard Sorel boot box to provide percussion accompaniment for the family's music performances. She enjoyed an Upper Peninsula childhood on Fire Lake, rich in freedom and exploration as she and her brother learned the ways of nature along the rivers and in the woods of Iron County; those experiences formed the core of her later varied musical accomplishments.

LAUREL PREMO

What a joy and rare privilege it has been for us and fellow *White Water* groupies to watch Laurel (and her brother, Evan) grow and flourish into accomplished musicians. Laurel currently is a graduate of the University of Michigan in the Performing Arts Technology Program, with specialty in Media Arts. Now a tall, slim young woman with graceful posture, a classically pretty oval face and a halo of curly light brown hair, she attracts admiring glances wherever she goes.

One afternoon when *White Water* was on the way to an evening concert in Manistique, Laurel alighted from the family van at a convenience store to purchase a can of soda. A young man walking in the opposite direction, watching her instead of where he was going, walked headlong into a gas pump—but he still was smiling (and looking) when he picked himself up.

Laurel's appeal is not just cosmetic. She plays almost every musical instrument known to western civilization: guitar, dobro, cittern, violin, banjo, Irish drum—the list goes on. To say she plays marvelously is too feeble a description; when Laurel performs she *is* the music.

Laurel also composes music, both instrumental and vocal. One of our favorite pieces is *The Veery*, a delightful tune that reminds us of this small woodland thrush, singing its lovely spiraling song on a warm evening. *The Veery* is included in Laurel's first CD, *Innertwine*, on which she sings and plays many of her own pieces. Did we mention that Laurel sings too? Some singing. One winter day a group of Celts were lured down a snowy path to the Chocolay River by her haunting rendition of "Down to the River."

It is easy to exhaust our supply of superlatives when describing this young woman. She also is a skilled graphic artist. Using colors, textures and forms, she creates a myriad of fantastic patterns, including the design for her new CD, *Stung by the Nettle*. This CD features thirteen original songs composed in several places around the world.

> "My name is Laurel Premo. I am driven to find notes and strings, to create with others, and to create for others. The music shouts and

> *murmurs life; the songs have been written in Helsinki, Fire Lake, Ann Arbor and water-soaked basements"* *

*www. laurelpremo.com

And that's not all: Laurel also writes—two of her stories were published in the *Marquette Monthly* before she graduated from Forest Park High School in Crystal Falls.

In the fall of 2008, Laurel traveled to Helsinki, Finland to study at the Sibelius Academy of Music, with special emphasis on folk music. It was a temporary loss to her family, to the *White Water* band and her many fans, but it was clear that she would be a fine ambassador from our region to that part of the world. Showing more temerity than a proper sense of humility, I cannot resist saying—and not in a shy way—that Laurel adopted this very blessed writer as her surrogate grandfather. My cup of joy runneth over.

There is a goodly supply of other human treasures in the Upper Peninsula—musicians, painters, potters, writers, story tellers—and a myriad of others who do the daily work that keeps this Superior Peninsula running. We celebrate them all; they are as much a part of the fabric that creates and maintains the special way of life in the north as are its natural treasures.

William Hamilton

INVESTMENTS IN SUMMER

"For I was rich, if not in money, in sunny hours and summer days."
—Henry David Thoreau

An Upper Peninsula summer is a superb time to make some investments. Not to worry, we don't mean ephemeral stocks or bonds. No Ponzi scheme here. Rather, we suggest investments in the incomparable beauty of summer—the greatest, longest-lasting "show"—Alma Nature.

The cost of these investments is minimal: some time, a bit of shoe leather, maybe an insect bite or two (or three). But the payoff, the return on your investment, is enormous. As with most things about nature, Thoreau said it best:

"No run on my bank can drain it, for my wealth is not in possessions but enjoyment."

During the bitter cold and dark days of January, while enduring the burden of a boring meeting (sorry for the redundancy there), or when the quiet desperation of daily chores gets you down, there is an escape. Call on the memories of summer and transport yourself to a warm, sunny oasis. Surprisingly, the brain does not recognize the difference between a real and an imagined image.

Opportunities for summer investments are all about us in this pleasant peninsula: the slopes of Mt. Marquette, the school forest off Forestville Road, the Elliott Donnelley tract on the Little Garlic River, Twin Waterfalls Nature Preserve in Munising, Harlow Lake and Little Presque Isle, Craig Lake Wilderness State Park, Portage Point, the myriad of lakes and rivers in the Hiawatha and Ottawa National Forests—only a few of our favorites.

What is on *your* list of favorite places and times? Each sensitive observer has favorite images of summer. Here are some we return to again and again; use them as stepping stones for your own path of discovery:

• The sight and sound of water is always soothing to those who take the time to sit quietly near our beautiful lakes, rivers and waterfalls. Try this: rest beside a waterfall and open your senses. Soak up the sounds of cascading water; taste the mist that swirls around you. Feel the power of water gruffing on the rocks. Some research indicates that such moving water produces negative ions, which reduce feelings of discomfort and anxiety. Or, perhaps "we're drawn to them (waterfalls) simply because they make us feel good" (Jerry Dennis, *The Bird in the Waterfall*).

• Have you looked at clouds from all sides lately? Find a grassy spot to lie on your back and let your mind drift along with the fluffy white pillows. Send yourself back to your childhood when you found all manner of fanciful shapes in those clouds scudding overhead.

• Spend some quiet time one late afternoon in a nearby hardwood forest. Watch the shifting patterns of light and shadow as the slanting rays of sunlight filter through the leaves of maple, oak, birch and basswood trees.

Although not necessary, some observers keep a journal and describe what they have seen and enjoyed. It may help to evoke memories you can turn to in colder, grayer times. Keep in mind that if an outdoor adventure is approached with an open mind and heart, then surely as night follows day, beauty, wonder and quiescence are sure to follow.

Here are three observations that started out as entries in my nature journal:

"Because they are the first splashes of green to emerge after the long winterscape, I am a fan of mossy logs. This past summer, motivated by local flora expert Virginia Foreman's gentle prodding, I examined patches of moss up close and personal. With your eyes at ground level—it's amazing—the stems of moss resemble a dense rain forest. I marveled at the interesting textures and the several shades of green."

"While examining a thick, luxurious tuft of moss growing in a crack on a sandstone ledge near Lake Superior, I yelped aloud in discovery: A colony of Sundew, an insect-eating plant, was growing in the moss. Each stalk was topped by a spatulate-shaped blade, each oval blade was covered with tiny hairs, and each hair was topped by a tiny drop of sticky liquid resembling dew. The slanting afternoon sun made the dewdrops into a bed of shimmering jewels."

"My favorite, though, is Caribou moss. Actually, it's not really a moss but a form of lichen, a primitive plant." You may have seen clinging to the surface of rocks. Caribou moss also grows abundantly in large patches on the ground, particularly in Jack Pine forests. See if you can find patches of it at Little Presque Isle. How many colors can you identify? Can you tell why it's called Caribou moss?

"We are all drawn to the movement of water. Something deep in our being compels us to watch waves marching toward land—is it the soothing rhythm?" Have you ever actually listened to combers as they reach the shore? Can you discern the several sounds which make up the water symphony? To get started, check out a book by Henry Beston: *The Outermost House*. Beston describes three basic sounds that occur as waves meet the land:

– a spilling crash as the wave churns up on land

– rapidly followed by a roar as the water expends its energy on the shore

– and then a hissing sound as the wave slides back

All of these acoustic effects are mingled as waves overlap and race for the shoreline. If you are patient, you will begin to detect a pattern, the elements of a water concert. Could it be the pulse of the planet?

"He doesn't have an extraordinary song, his plumage is not exotic or even particularly colorful, and he lives unobtrusively close to the ground, but I expect this small bird nests close to your house or cabin while he goes about the business of making a living largely unnoticed." Let me introduce the friendly chipping sparrow. He is named for the song: a simple, almost insect-like trill or chipping sound. He seems to say "chip-chip-chip . . . " very rapidly until it blurs into a dry buzz. I think it is a fine-looking bird—it has a perky rusty cap, a white eyebrow, a black line through its eye and a pearly gray chest. You will find the chippy almost anywhere except in dense forests. This sparrow likes brushy areas and often nests in low bushes near homes and gardens. See if a family of chipping sparrows lives close to you.

In the Navajo language there is an expression, *hozhoo*, which means to seek harmony and balance by walking gently and with reverence on the earth—they call this the Beauty Way. We, as non-natives, have to work harder because our lifestyle and social institutions are designed to separate and buffer us from nature. For many, nature is simply a barrier, a force to subdue rather than a subject of wonderment. Let us strive to overcome this estrangement and get on speaking terms with our small portion of the earth.

"The real voyage of discovery consists not in seeking new landscapes but in having new eyes." –Marcel Proust

If an outdoor adventure is approached with an open mind and heart, then surely beauty, wonder and quiescence are sure to follow. When we cultivate awareness of the natural world, it awakens ancient memories which help us calibrate our present lives. After a walk in forest or field, even if only as a stroll down memory lane, we always feel better. These investments guarantee dividends.

William Hamilton

THE LEGACY OF LAND

*I*t is late summer in the Upper Peninsula of Michigan and Jack Frost has been nipping at the maples. The forest is going about the annual metamorphosis and I, too, am transformed; there is a subtle flavor of melancholy, a lingering reverie of long summer days and carefree vacation memories.

I pause to rest on a steep ridge where Lynn has erected a simple wooden sign in memory of my mother. As I sit amid the late summer foliage of the land my mother's bequest allowed us to purchase, I feel her reaching out in love one last time. So overcome am I by the ache of years long gone that I have to sit down and lean back against the rough bark of a maple tree. I muse for a long time remembering how much Mother loved the north.

Born in Calumet near the turn of the twentieth century, Gertrude Mary Harris Emerick was a daughter of the Upper Peninsula. In her youth, her heart was claimed by this beautiful peninsula and her passion for Lake Superior, the flinty hills and dense forests never diminished. She felt—even as I now feel—blessed with the opportunity to dwell in a unique and wondrous land. The rugged peninsula shaped and defined her life, for it was here, in the place where she was born, that she first connected with the earth.

My mother's forebears came from Cornwall, a remote duchy of highly independent Celts in the far west of England. Cornwall is, in many respects, a lot like the Upper Peninsula—a blend of rock, water and vast expanses of green. The Cornish are great bakers, sing like angels and were known worldwide as prodigious copper miners. When ore was discovered in the Keweenaw Peninsula, a rocky finger of granite which curves out into Lake Superior, the call went out for hardrock Cornish miners. In some cases, other workers refused to enter a mine unless led and supervised by a "Cousin Jack," a label given to men from Cornwall. They always seemed to have another cousin back in the old country when additional miners were needed.

It was a time of great ore discoveries in Michigan. Mother's ancestors came first to Central Mine in 1850 and then followed the work to copper boom towns like Mohawk, Ahmeek and for the longest period, at the Great (the adjective was always used) Calumet and Hecla operation. The Copper Country, as it came to be called, was thriving.

My mother loved the life in Calumet. Despite the harsh climate and isolation, the city crackled with growth. The area population toped 100,000 and they had all the amenities, including a new opera house featuring performers such as John Sousa, Lillian Russell and Sarah Bernhardt. But it all came asunder on July 23, 1913, when 13,000 miners went on strike for better working conditions. Violence erupted and the National Guard was called in. Gertrude's father, my grandfather Harris, was by this time the undersheriff and by duty was allied with the authorities trying to impose order. The tension was extreme and finally exploded into tragedy during the holiday season. On Christmas Eve, more than 400 miners and their families were attending a party on the upper floor of the Italian Hall when someone shouted "Fire!" In a frenzy, the crowd rushed down the long stairs, stumbled and piled in a heap in the narrow stairwell. Sixty-two children and eleven adults died of suffocation in the resultant crush. There had been no fire. My mother remembered watching the long, sad funeral cortege of small coffins winding its way through the center of the town.

To escape the hostility—Mother also remembered threats at school and bullets coming through the windows of their home—the family moved to White Pine, a small village near the site of the future Porcupine Mountains Wilderness State Park. Here she lived an idyllic outdoor life with sledding and skiing in the winter and picking berries, fishing and swimming in the summer. The Lake Superior beach was nearby and there were miles of remote country paradise for young children to explore.

Economic times, though, were hard in the Upper Peninsula. In order to provide a better life for his family, my grandfather moved again, this time to Detroit where he worked for many decades for the Ford Motor Company. Gertrude married, raised four sons and became a grandmother. She built a life in a suburb of Detroit. Days, months, years slipped by.

Yet she always felt like an exile in the cities far from her beloved North Country. The occasional visit to the Copper Country only served to magnify the gulf between the suburban lifestyle and the space and solitude of the land up north. Her memories of her early life remained vivid. In her eighty-second summer I took her to the Cornish reunion held each July at the ghost town of Central Mine. Later we stopped in front of the ancestral home in Calumet. While we stood gazing at the undistinguished company house she had lived in so long ago, an old man slowly ambled past. "Jerry Murphy!" my mother shouted in glee. She had recognized him as a classmate from more than seventy years before!

Later, my mother understood when I spurned offers from prestigious universities in the Midwest and chose a teaching position at the much smaller Northern Michigan University. In the four decades since, I have never regretted taking the path less traveled. I am exactly where I was meant to be—in the land where my mother began.

All the while my family was reveling in the Upper Peninsula good life, Mother was quietly assembling a small legacy to leave to her sons. For many years she worked long hours at Kresge stores and put her wages into stock in what later became K-Mart. Its substantial growth must have been a poignant pleasure to someone who had endured the privations of the Great Depression. I was astonished and very touched when the check arrived following the settlement of her estate.

What could I do with the unexpected bequest that would serve as a tribute to this daughter of the Upper Peninsula? I didn't need more things, there were too many to keep track of already. It took only a few minutes to find just the right answer: land.

My mother and I had shared a devotion to this harsh and beautiful place. So we would obtain land near our home in West Branch Township, a dozen miles south of the Lake Superior shore. The township has huge farm fields, gorgeous upland forests and winding rivers.

It seems many of us are looking for a place, a spot where we feel a sense of home, of belonging. Thus it was with our Foster Creek Homestead. When we found the land, there was an immediate and compelling sense of happiness and peace.

The forty acres that we were able to purchase with the help of Mother's legacy has high wooded ridges, maple and conifer groves, a small open meadow with a carpet of wildflowers and most of all, a strong sense of Mother's approval for our choice. We know we do not truly "own" the land, but are deeply pleased to be its caretakers for future generations.

I feel my mother's long exile is over and her spirit is back among these lovely ridges and valleys. Emerson wrote that "the mind loves its old home." A daughter of the Upper Peninsula has finally come home.

Photo: Mark Mitchell

Autumn

Mark Mitchell

Mark Mitchell

Lon Emerick

Mark Mitchell

108 AUTUMN

Autumn
INTRODUCTION

Autumn is a many-splendored season in the Upper Peninsula, an interlude of raucous colors, aromas, harvest moons and frantic activity as nature gets ready for the next act in the annual cycle: winter, the defining season in our northern paradise. Since our fall is fleeting, we must be outdoors to savor it before the arrival of the long white and cold.

One of the best times of day to enjoy our brief autumn is during the gloamin'. Sally forth in late evening "when the light is dim and low and quiet shadows falling" (Annie Harrison).

This last period of dusk or twilight is a magical interlude for discovery. The light angling through the trees touches all around more softly; the woods and waters seem to hush as night approaches. Look for little things—a late blooming flower, a single red leaf. Emerson wrote that the . . . "an invariable mark of wisdom is to see the miraculous in the common."

Almost anywhere is good for a twilight ramble, but we usually seek out an edge, a place where two ecological communities meet (an ecotone); a dense forest adjoining an open field; an old roadway through a savannah; a marsh surrounded by tamarack trees.

Walk very slowly and stop often; to cover 100 yards in fifteen minutes is a good pace. Here are just a few of the delights we encountered early one recent autumn evening while moseying along Yalmer Road in Skandia:

• A flight of white-throated sparrows was assembling for the annual migration to a warmer clime. We counted at least a dozen birds feeding quickly. Most songbirds travel at night, guided by the stars, and they must stoke up for the long trip. Tomorrow morning they probably will be in Ohio.

- We scuffed through some downed aspen leaves and the rich organic aroma of autumn rose to grace our every step. This is the signature smell of the forest in fall woods And all those leaves provide an immense crop of nutrients to the soil. Outdoor writer John Bates described the considerable value of downed leaves:

> "While a maple leaf weighs barely a fiftieth of an ounce, the total dry leaf-fall on one acre of mixed-maple woods contains around 1½ tons of free nutrients and organic matter every year."

- Stopping under a red maple tree, we marveled, as we do each fall, at the crimson glow. Even in the twilight, the splendor is reflected and amplified by hundreds of brilliantly glowing surfaces. Thoreau phrased it more artfully:

> "...the woods glow through the green, yellow and scarlet, like fires just kindled . . . a general conflagration just fairly underway, soon to envelop every tree."

- Look over there, on the edge of the old field: a crowd of blue asters and pearly everlasting, almost the last actors in the seasonal drama of flowers. See how the ranks of goldenrod—frosty silver now—try to hold the stage.

As we made our way back to our vehicle, we stopped to watch thin wisps of mist rising from the fallow field. What a calm and restful way to end a day.

When asked about his apparent vigorous health, an elderly Cornishman (G.M. Trevelyan) responded: "I have two doctors, my left leg and my right . . . when I walk my thoughts start out with me like bloodstained mutineers debauching themselves on board the ship, but when I bring them home at nightfall, they are larking and tumbling over each other like happy little boy scouts at play."

So, we urge you now to go roamin' in the gloamin'—and hum a tune in honor of Harry Lauder, Scottish singer, who made the phrase his own. Savor these last fragments of autumn before the North Country enters the long white slumber.

Sites we return to in the fall:

- The old railroad bed by Harlow Lake—take the walk to the granite overlook above Harlow Lake for sweeping views of the forest and lake.
- Sand Point Marsh boardwalk (Munising). This is a good place to see migrating birds—rough-legged hawks and snow buntings come south to the U.P. for winter!
- Days River Pathway (Gladstone)
- Redwyn Dunes Natural Area (Eagle Harbor)
- The Sturgeon River Slough just south of Chassell
- Lake Michigan boardwalk (Manistique)

- Mt. Marquette's granite overlooks
- Bruno's Run Trail along the Indian River (Hiawatha National Forest, Hwy 13, south of Wetmore).
- Stonington Peninsula in Delta County—you might catch the migration of Monarch butterflies to their winter home in Mexico.

William Hamilton

IN PRAISE OF GOLDENROD

It is mid-September and all across the Upper Peninsula the glorious roadside show of wildflowers is almost finished. Now in my travels along country roads in central Marquette County, I see asters blowing in the wind and rank upon rank of purple: the invasive pest, spotted knapweed. Alas, the color purple reminds me that the academic year at the University will soon commence; I am reluctant to break the pattern of summer roaming free.

But then I find gold: my favorite flower, goldenrod. I look forward all summer to the waves of bright yellow decorating all the roads and abandoned fields. Many years ago, enamoured of the simple beauty of the goldenrod plant, I looked up the flower in various botanical references. After I discovered that there are some sixty-nine varieties, and that it is often difficult to tell one from the other, I decided I would rather spend my time admiring its beauty than keying down which variety I happened to be adoring at the moment.

This native plant is a vigorous seeder. It sprouts in late May and early June along our rural road. I watch it growing rapidly into tall (two to four feet high), healthy groups with dark stems and lance-like leaves. When the Joe Pye weed flowers in August, with its signature large flat top of purple/grey, my anticipation heightens because I know the first blooms of goldenrod are soon to follow.

The goldenrod is a member of the daisy family, termed composites because of the many small flowers growing together. Large clusters of yellow florets that look a bit like a pile carpet sprout in all directions. Insects, including platoons of bees, flock to the blossoms to gather the last nectar and pollen of the year. As the chill of autumn appears, I see dozens of bumble bees clinging upside down on the plumes of gold.

Another insect, the goldenrod gall fly, uses the stem of the plant for a nursery of sorts. After laying its eggs on the sturdy stems, the larvae hatch and begin feeding on the plant. The plant responds by forming a roundish, hard capsule—it looks a lot like an onion set. This provides the larvae, now in the pupa stage, a secure home for the winter. But two other opportunistic creatures know this and use the insect for their own purposes. The Downy Woodpecker drills into the hard capsule and is rewarded with a winter snack. Local ice fishermen open the capsule and use the developing insect to entice a fish for a winter fish fry.

Some human observers take umbrage at my love affair with the goldenrod plant, complaining that it provokes allergies. I gently point out that it is the plant's cousin, ragweed, which is the main agent of upper respiratory discomfort in the fall.

In fact, one variety of goldenrod, sweet goldenrod, was used a tonic for general malaise. A tea was brewed—it has an anise flavor—and administered to the sick person. I could find no information to determine if patients got better after drinking the goldenrod tonic or feigned recovery to thwart further doses.

Goldenrod grows in dense clusters and does not suffer other plants gladly. It releases an enzyme from its roots that discourages competing vegetation from sprouting nearby.

Sometime in October, the plant trades its golden tresses for a crown of silver-grey. Even when elderly, the goldenrod is an attractive and distinguished plant. I like the way George Peale described this transformation in the sixteenth century:

"His golden locks hath turned to silver."

Long after other plants have withered and fallen, the goldenrod stands tall on stout stems, even through the winter snows. The hardy plant continues to "pay it forward" all winter. Its small seeds are prized by chickadees, goldfinches and snow buntings. Goldenrod has been one of my favorite role models.

What I learned from goldenrod

1. Bloom where you are planted

2. Cast your net widely

3. Be flexible, adaptable to life's exigencies

4. Provide a harbor of refuge for others

5. Pass along your bounty—pay it forward

6. Celebrate the seasons with color and joy

7. Be loyal to family and friends; stand together

8. Age with grace

9. Turn adversity into a useful outcome

10. Bide your time; persistence is more effective than haste

DIAMONDS ARE FOREVER

After a chilly summer in the Upper Peninsula, with winds sometimes reaching gale force, accompanied by temperatures that cancelled out camping plans, community festivals and beach days, here came September.

The patience of residents who "winter in place," a patience which had been sorely tested as they waited for the warmer days of usual summers, was rewarded with soft breezes, sunny days and balmy evenings.

It was enough to make a year-round "Yooper" positively giddy and driven to spend as much time as possible outdoors in this lovely land before the return of the long white.

An author whose name I have forgotten wrote that if we are fortunate in our lives, we will have a few times he called "diamonds"—peak experiences so memorable, so out of the quotidian pace of life, that they add a new dimension to our lives and stay with us long after the time has passed.

On a September evening, one of those diamond times came for us at a granite-rimmed lake deep in national forest lands in a western Upper Peninsula county. Invited by friends to share an evening of walking, fishing and companionship, we arrived for an early evening picnic after a long drive from our home near Skandia. As we admired the lake and surrounding forest from our dinner perch on shore, a trout rose, making perfect circles on the still surface. Then a mature bald eagle flew down the length of the lake, the late afternoon sun lighting up the distinctive white of its head and tail feathers.

A trio of wood ducks followed the curve of the shoreline as they returned to their nighttime resting place. We felt we had seen enough to fill our senses when a great blue heron—so silently—coasted above us. As we pushed out on to the lake in a small boat, a loon called, and a beaver repeatedly sounded its tail-slapping alarm call at our intrusion, first from one side of the lake, and it seemed almost immediately, from the other shoreline. As far as we could tell, there was only one individual on patrol. How did it cross the lake so swiftly?

BALD EAGLE AT WILDERNESS LAKE

As we moved down the middle of the lake, trying to guess the direction of the feeding trout and cast just ahead of their pattern, another bald eagle landed in a white pine above us. It turned its head from side to side, almost as if posing for the photos we took. Of course, its head-turning moves were using keen eyesight to search for fish, and we later did see it swoop, catch a trout and rise off the lake with its meal firmly secured.

It really was almost too much—and then the full moon rose over the far end of the lake and cast a silver path toward us. As if on cue, several wolves started to howl. The howling only lasted for a few minutes, but we were transfixed by hearing the distinctive sounds so evocative of wilderness.

That September evening, surrounded by the sounds and sights of the natural world we still can find here in the Upper Peninsula, was a diamond experience we will long remember.

And here's the thing: It is not always necessary to travel to some remote environ to enjoy a peak experience in the natural world. Seek some quiet place close to home and make it your island of renewal.

• Go to your haven often. Make yourself familiar with the tree bark, the smell of leaf mold, how the seasons alter the place. In his book *The Path,* Chet Raymo offers some guidelines: "Any path can become *The* Path if attended to with care, without preconceptions, informed by knowledge and open to surprise."

• Still your inner voice. Leave your work-a-day life at home or in your vehicle. At those times when I am bedeviled by the work ethic—that I *should be doing something productive*—I scribble my thanks to the Puritans and then toss the paper in the trunk.

• Remember that it takes time to shed the layers of work, worry and care. Heed the worlds of John Muir: "I only went out for a walk and finally concluded to stay until sundown, for going *out,* I found, was really going *in*."

With some wording changes to an old standard song: "deep in the winter, try to remember the kind of September when life was slow and oh, so mellow . . . when grass was green and grain was yellow . . . " ("Try to Remember" lyrics by Tom Jones, 1960)

What "diamonds" have you stored for later memories?

THE GOLDEN CROWN

Now comes the brief, extravagant season of autumn color. For a few shining days in October, nature startles us with a dramatic reminder of the inevitable cycle of seasons. There is no understatement in a north country fall; all flags are flying at journey's end. The message is shouted out: summer is dead, winter is coming.

We know, of course, that the resplendent hues of fall have been residing dormant all along, hidden by the green of chlorophyl during the growing season. Then, as days grow shorter and colder, the tree shuts off the water supply to the leaves and the deep green foliage fades, exposing the myriad shades of red and yellow. Many trees turn exactly the same color each year. Sugar maples seem to favor shades of yellow although I have seen them dressed in orange, peach, even bright red. On my favorite hiking path, two elderly maples grow side by side. Each fall, one turns bright yellow and its neighbor always assumes a red-orange hue. The inveterate leaf-looker can depend upon red maples.

If days are sunny and the nights chilly, the leaves of some species go on making sugar until all the chlorophyl is gone (temperatures below forty-five degrees slow down the removal of sugar from a leaf). Young oaks often do this and the resultant extra sugar reacts with the minerals to create deep carmine and purple. The autumn forest appears to have been painted with bold, broad strokes by an artist whose brush has run wild in bright and startling colors.

Although the visitor can behold the annual charms of an Upper Peninsula autumn in any portion of the region and every lonely backwoods road becomes a fantasy land, we find ourselves returning again and again to areas where we can see the colorful leaves against a backdrop of water. The rolling expanse of flinty hills surrounding Lake of the Clouds in the Porcupine Mountains, the vista from Brockway Mountain in the Copper Country or the view from Sugar Loaf and Marquette Mountain draw us back again each October.

Regardless of where you go, all the forest has a special luminous quality in autumn, an open resplendent character which contrasts sharply with the deep cool shadows of summer. The woods are lit up by the reflections of lights from thousands of brilliant yellow and red torches: those still decorating the trees, and others carpeting the ground.

Even on somber days in early fall, the gloriously colored leaves emit a pulsating glow which seems to flood the thickest glade and deepest valley. Countless times during a soft rain I have stood under a huge maple and marveled at the lustrous stream of light emanating from the wet leaves.

But all things bright and beautiful come to an end—how could we tolerate this leaf display all year? A few leaves detach and drift down right from the first hint of color. Then sometime between October 15 and 20, the colorful display descends in showers. If the weather is just right—frosty, but dry and with little breeze—you can witness the autumnal spectacle of thousands of golden leaves swimming on the air.

For many years now, in my capacity as self-appointed inspector of autumn mornings, I have attended the annual descent of color. One memorable time, on an old road near Addis Ponds, north of M-94 in the Hiawatha National Forest, I chanced to be sitting on a stump just when the leaves began to fall all around and on me. Stunned by the beauty of the golden leafy shower, I sat in reverent awe.

Then, remembering an old legend—that a person will have one month of good luck in the new year for each leaf caught in midair as it falls—I ran from place to place with outstretched hands until I had a year's supply of good fortune in the form of leafy bits of sunshine gold.

Exhilarated, I resumed my seat on the stump to soak in the marvel of the morning. Just then, one last large yellow leaf spiraled down and landed softly on my head. A golden crown for me on my wooden throne. As I sat there contemplating this wonder, I thought that I was distinguished more by this blessing of a simple yellow leaf than I would have been by all the jewels of British royalty. I wore the leaf all morning.

The deciduous trees—maples, birches, aspen and oaks—are the featured attractions of our annual autumn splendor. But conifers also shed some needles in the fall. Have you seen the sprinkling of golden-brown in the dense green foliage of white pine trees? It is more subdued but appealing none-the-less. On our Foster Creek Homestead there is a dense grove of mature white pines. Sitting on the soft layer of needles the trees have shed for many years, I lean against the bark of one particularly large pine and offer a prayer of thanks that this signature tree of the north still waves its lustrous green foliage in the wind.

Now, just when it seems as if the colorful spectacle of fall is over, another tree of the north unveils the last surprise before the landscape segues into shades of black and white. The tamarack, called larch in the western states, is a tree that has an identity crisis: It can't seem to make up its mind whether it's a conifer or a deciduous tree. It is, in fact, the only conifer that sheds all its needles in autumn. For a brief interval after the maples, birches and aspen have dropped their many-splendored raiment, tamaracks put on quite a show. Every wetland is dotted with a display of gold.

You can collect leaves, press them, photograph or paint them, but you cannot capture them. In the end you must simply experience them—to expand beauty in your soul and to be reminded that all things renew themselves in nature. Autumn is so short and yet so enthusiastic, so spectacular and so important to the endless circle of the seasons in the north country.

William Hamilton

CHICKADEE ON MY ARROW

It is a glorious autumn evening in mid-October and I am poised high up in a maple tree waiting expectantly for a whitetail deer to amble down a nearby runway. What a feast for the senses it is to sit here among the lemon and crimson leaves in the slanting rays of the sun. I drink in the wonderful aromas of fall ripeness and note with pleasure that the bird migration is in full swing. All the beauty turns a key in my consciousness that unlocks wonder, then joy and finally contentment.

Slowly I blend into the forest. Suddenly, a pert black-capped chickadee spirals in and lands on my arrow! The bird peers at me inquisitively—clad in camouflage I must look like a large irregular branch and for just a moment we are locked together in silent communion. "Chickadee-dee-dee" he lisps, more from confusion I suspect than by way of greeting. In an instant he is gone. But the magic lingers and I am transformed by this fleeting intimate connection with a wild creature.

I am soon to see it is only the beginning of the most wondrous evening afield I have experienced in more than a half-century of hunting. Layers of everyday life fall away and the hunt releases my body and captivates my mind and soul. I am suspended in a timeless pursuit, a direct, elemental and personal encounter with nature.

Leaning back against the maple's rough bark, I remember the question asked by a gentle woman at a dinner party last night: "Why do you hunt wild animals?" As most hunters know, lurking behind that inquiry is usually a negative opinion waiting for birth. So I was not surprised when the lady—who was daintily chewing a piece of meat—dismissed my halting answer with a wave and a jangle of her gold bracelets. "It's so, so, barbarian," she said before turning back to dissect her meat. I should have known better after all these years. Trying to share my passion for hunting with someone who has already made up her mind is a bit like trying to teach a pig to sing. It's a waste of your time—and it annoys the pig.

A wild, raucous calling interrupts my bemusing reverie. Barely three hundred feet overhead a flock of sandhill cranes is assembling for the annual fall migration.

The huge gray birds circle slowly, around and around, gaining altitude in search of a thermal that will carry them south with the night. Up and up they spiral, their rolling, high staccato voices becoming fainter and fainter.

So entranced am I by the flight of cranes that I have forgotten to scan the woods below my tree stand. I sense that some animal, probably a deer, is close by. Sure enough, a large buck has emerged from some spruces and is poised warily not more than twenty yards away. He is at full alert and raises his muzzle to winnow the air. His attention is focused not on me, however, but toward something on the ground nearby. The buck shifts anxiously for a better view, bobbing his head up and down the way alarmed deer do. Then abruptly, the deer bounds away in huge, graceful leaps, but doesn't go far. I can still see his white flag tail in the dense brush.

I am astonished to see a mature bobcat stalk into the clearing—the first time I have seen that fellow hunter in fifty years of hunting. The cat is tawny, heavily muscled and moves with taut grace. Instead of chasing the buck—perhaps he knows that his only opportunity was stealth and there is little chance he can catch an adult deer on the run—the bobcat disappears into a thicket. Only when the cat is gone do I realize I have been holding my breath and I let it out in a soft sigh of wonder.

The light is fading now and fingers of deep blue are creeping across the opening in the forest. I close my eyes briefly and savor the incredible evening I have spent perched in a tree. When I open my eyes for one last look, the buck has reappeared under my stand. The deer saunters closer and nibbles on an aspen twig. Shifting slightly, I raise my bow and align the ten-yard pin on a spot behind his shoulder. Then, I lower the bow and watch happily as the buck ambles out into a nearby alfalfa field.

TROPHY DEER

I smile and think of my grandfather. The old man got more pleasure out of being in the position to kill a deer than he did by actually taking one. Sometimes he would say something based on his reading of Robert Service: "Yet it isn't the deer that I'm wanting, so much as just finding the deer."

I must confess that when I was young I thought only of killing a whitetail buck. I simply could not understand my grandfather and his hunting partners. They were content to share the camp life and roam the woods. As I lurked impatiently in the forest, I told myself I would never be like that.

Well, now I am the grandfather and I have put away such thoughts. I realize that bagging a deer is only one small part, in some ways the least important part, of the annual hunting season. I believe, too, that for the future of hunting, we need to have genuine respect, even reverence, not only for the game we seek but for all of nature.

As I make my way back to camp in deep twilight, I can almost hear the gentle lady questioner commenting on my evening: "See," she might say with a bit of mockery in her voice, "you could have had the same experience in the woods with a camera." Perhaps. Yet then I am just an observer. With a weapon I am a participant in the ancient drama of life. We are so isolated and insulated from nature in our modern lives that it is easy to conclude that humans are excluded from natural processes. The art of pursuing game reminds me that all creatures are interconnected in the web of life. Even though I have decided not to kill an animal any more, when I hunt I am responding to the tug of an ancient ritual embedded deeply in the human genome—and I rediscover a comforting continuity with my heritage.

Coda

More Upper Peninsula magic awaited me on the drive from Rock to my home in Skandia. There, as if beckoning me, a brilliant display of Northern Lights. Eerie vertical streamers of green, pale yellow and white danced on the horizon.

When I entered the house, Lynn asked as she always does, "Did you see anything?" "Let me tell you!" I replied.

William Hamilton

DISCOVERING: THE U.P. ANTHEM

The State of Michigan has an official song, but it has not been accorded status as *the* official song. "My Michigan" by Kavanagh and Clint features (in our view) some rather archaic and cloying lyrics. A more popular song, "Michigan, My Michigan" was first written by Winifred Lister of Detroit in 1862 and sung to the tune of "O Tannenbaum, O Tannenbaum." Both the words and the music have been changed by several authors and lyricists over the years.

Fortunately, those of us who are privileged to dwell above the bridge have our very own anthem, and it expresses exactly how we feel about the Upper Peninsula. If you have not heard the song, tune in to *Discovering* with Buck LeVasseur at 7:30 on Monday evenings on local channel TV6.

The signature song was composed by renaissance man, Mark Mitchell. A longtime resident, he is a multi-talented artist: in addition to composing and performing music, he creates exquisite pieces in leather, metal, wood. Mitchell knew during early childhood he was destined to be an artist; he was drawing constantly. After a very brief period of training in engineering, he earned a BA in Fine Arts at Wayne State University and a Master's degree in Fine Arts from the prestigious Cranbrook Institute in Bloomfield Hills.

Following his formal education, Mitchell made a wise and life-changing move: he came north to the Superior Peninsula, found forty acres of wooded land, built three log cabins there and began a long love affair with the U.P. He maintains the natural world motivates his art and sustains his life in a myriad of ways.

Many local residents know of Mitchell as a singer/songwriter. He has produced several albums of his original songs. All of his music celebrates the beauty of the Upper Peninsula and the work of loggers, miners and fishermen who built a place for us in this land. He has performed in venues all over Michigan.

For several years, Mitchell was a political cartoonist for the Mining Journal in Marquette. Have you seen his photographs? Superb images of ice crystals, a

MARK MITCHELL IN STUDIO

milkweed pod in the act of springing open, an entire portfolio of Little Presque Isle in all seasons—all lovingly portrayed in stunning color. One of his Little Presque Isle framed photos hangs on a wall in our own log home. Looking north from near Freeman's Landing, his camera has captured the point and the offshore island; it evokes for us the special beauty of this place along the Lake Superior shoreline. I am honored that Mark has agreed to have several of his beautiful, iconic Upper Peninsula photographs in *Paradise North*.

Recently, Mitchell has focused on his first artistic love: sculpting wood. His creations may be seen at the Studio Gallery in Marquette and at the Miskwabik Gallery in Calumet.

We leave you now with the lyrics from Mark Mitchell's *Discovering* song, which celebrates our natural heritage—the forests, Great Lakes and wildlife of the Upper Peninsula.

> *"The secret streams that flow beneath the cliffs of colored stone*
> *The forests thick and healthy with birch and pine and oak*
> *Surrounded by the greatest lakes this world has ever known*
>
> *The black bear's awesome presence as he roams the hills and fields*
> *The call of the timber wolf, the loon's lonesome trill*
> *The eagle soaring high above, the trout lies deep and still*
>
> *Chorus:*
> *These are what I treasure, the only way I measure*
> *The feelings that I have for this fine land*
> *There is so much to discover when you're a long time lover*
> *Of Northern Michigan*
>
> *The ghostly silent passing of the white tail in the dawn*
> *The silver flashing salmon on their yearly spawning run*
> *The chorus of the northern geese beneath an autumn sun*

The customs and the people from a dozen foreign lands
The years of toil that's written in their faces, on their hands
The children's laugh, the women's strength, the courage of the men

Chorus:
These are what I treasure, the only way I measure
The feelings that I have for this fine land
There is so much to discover when you're a long time lover
Of Northern Michigan

© Mark Mitchell

William Hamilton

A GATHERING IN THE FOREST

It is 5:00 a.m., November 15, and all through U.P. deer camps, the hunters are stirring with not even a moan. The chef-of-the-day rose even earlier to prepare breakfast and now he awakens the slumbering crew with the traditional cry: "Daylight in the swamp!" The delightful aroma of pancakes, hash browns, bacon and eggs provokes the nimrods to hustle. No one wants to be late on opening day of deer season.

Deer Camp: What a host of mental images that simple phrase evokes. Never have so few words produced so many memories for so many persons. In the Upper Peninsula, of course, the firearm deer season is a singularly important event. Indeed, November 15—OPENING DAY—assumes the aura of a holy day of obligation for so many men and women that business, education, even health care all take a temporary sabbatical.

When the deer season begins this year, it will mark sixty years of opening days for me. Although I have been in scores of hunting camps during the past half-century, the images of the very first season at my grandfather's cabin are deeply imprinted in my consciousness. As the Old Man's favorite grandson, I was invited to learn to hunt at camp with his three partners—all older, retired nimrods. It was made abundantly clear to me that I was the plebe. They all referred to me as "The Lad" and assigned me many chores as part of my initiation rite. "The Lad can do that," or "Let the Lad do this," the elderly hunters observed with some delight as they got out the cards for an ongoing game of poker. I carried water, brought in firewood, washed the dishes and was a general aide-de-camp for the week.

It was, to say the least, a challenging week for a teenager. The food was unfamiliar (nondescript stews) and heavily spiced. With the loud chorus of snoring each night, it was almost impossible to sleep even with a pillow over my head.

Yet I loved it. Never had I felt so ablaze with life. I had become a deer hunter. And now, sixty years later, in spite of cold feet, sore muscles and sleep deprivation, I still hunger for deer season. The exhilaration I feel in the autumn forest is worth every bit of discomfort. What nourishes such an obsession?

Anticipation

How delicious and exciting it is to plan the annual event—for many of us, it accounts for at least half the pleasure of deer hunting. Simple activities like checking the red clothing, oiling the gun and sharpening the knife are sensuous rituals which resonate deeply in a hunter's spirit. And of course the hunting talk: the endless dissection of past adventures and extravagant predictions for future accomplishments.

Deer Camp

In my travels down remote byways, I have admired scores of hunting camps. Each camp has a devoted group of hunters who consider it deer season heaven. Simply thinking about the camp excites them beyond comprehension. Those of us who dwell in the Upper Peninsula are so fortunate: We are always close to camp. At the slightest excuse, we can head for the woods to do those little chores that add to the excitement as opening day approaches: oil lamps to fill, wood to split, shelves to stock with provisions, the buck pole to be inspected and hunting sites scouted.

Camaraderie

What a wonderfully diverse group of characters comes together to pursue the whitetail deer in a spirit of friendly good-fellowship each autumn. When I was the Lad in my grandfather's deer camp, I sometimes thought that his partners were a bunch of grumpy old men who basically disliked each other. Now I know better. Despite the complaints, the insults, the zingers—or maybe because of them—they all looked forward to seeing each other in November.

Although retired from active pursuit of whitetail deer, I still feel the tug of opening day excitement. But sixty years is enough—it has been, as they say, a good ride. Even more enduring than the trophies on the wall or the venison meatloaf, is a treasure trove of memories that ride gentle on my mind.

It is the amusing incidents afield that offer the most lasting and vivid recollections. By some strange quirk of fate, or perhaps due to a zany temperament, a number of peculiar events have occurred during my hunting adventures. Among all the humorous tales, this is my favorite because it is not only amusing but reflects how serious we are about our deer hunting:

The members of the Kernow Camp had hunted together for many happy years. They were all getting a bit long in the tooth and most of them were nursing various ailments. Instead of hunting alone, they decided to pair up so that if someone had a problem, his partner could summon help.

Old Bernie Medlyn, who had been through some heart troubles, was paired with his good buddy, Harvey Treloar, and on opening day they went up to a new deer blind on the Salmon Trout River.

It was almost dark when Harvey struggled back into camp dragging a beautiful eight-point buck. All the old guys ran out of the cabin to admire Harvey's deer. It was the best whitetail buck taken at Kernow Camp in many years and Harvey basked in all the praise and awe. When the excitement had settled down, Alex Pentreath asked, "Say, Harvey, where's Bernie?"

Harvey looked down at his deer and then up at the circle of his long-time hunting buddies. "Well, guys, Bernie got real sick after lunch . . . and he died," Harvey said.

There was a collective audible sigh of shock and disbelief.

"But Harvey," Alex said incredulously, "you dragged this here buck back to camp and left Bernie in the woods?"

Harvey took off his blaze orange Stormy Kromer hat, looked down admiringly at his eight-point buck and replied, "No one's going to steal Bernie."

The men looked at each other, nodded in agreement and filed back into the camp to have a celebratory drink to Harvey's successful hunt.

KERNOW CAMP

William Hamilton

THE GALES OF NOVEMBER

It was obvious: I needed to get away from the speech clinic following a lengthy treatment program for an adult with a severe stuttering problem. With a team of graduate student interns, I had been working almost around the clock with Jesse for six weeks—in addition to teaching classes, dealing with departmental issues and the inevitable university committee meetings. The client was ecstatic at what he had accomplished and was ready to return to his life in Chicago. We, the therapy team, were exhilarated but exhausted.

Remembering the therapists' dictum about the imperative of the clinician's mental hygiene—you can't heal a wound with a dirty bandage—team members sought their own prescriptions for recharging their batteries. And so, late Friday morning, I loaded supplies into my truck and headed to our remote log cabin, the AuTrain Hermitage. It was November 14, the day before the opening of the annual deer hunting season. The wearing of red (now blaze orange) is just as significant a gesture as observing St. Patrick's Day green. At least I had a legitimate excuse to cover my absence from the university.

The AuTrain Hermitage is my healing site. Located on the shore of Lake Superior in an isolated and remote area, it is a perfect place for eliminating work-a-day stress. It is a place to roam without a destination, blend into the dense forest, and listen to the silence. Most of all, it meant no words after six weeks of endless dialogue, planning sessions, treatment encounters, evaluations and writing reports.

Almost immediately after I opened the door to the log structure and smelled the aroma of cedar and wood smoke from countless fires, I began to unwind. Doing small chores helped me slide further into a deep comfort zone. I built a fire in the wood burning stove (kindling and birchbark are always ready). After eating a Cornish pasty and savoring a cup of camomile tea, I spent some time admiring the immense blue of Lake Superior.

There is always a cache of books meant to be read in a remote cabin. With only the soft guttering of a wood fire for background music, I reclined on a soft couch and revisited Thoreau's *Walden*. In a state of grace I blew out the oil lamps and went to bed at 7 p.m. thinking how fortunate I am to have this AuTrain hideaway. Even Lake Superior was quiet.

I woke up to a November gale on the Big Lake. Strong winds out of the northwest buffeted the cabin and spray from the Lake covered the porch and coated the windows. Superior was in a boiling frenzy.

As I watched the autumn fury, I remembered the statistics: In late October and early November there have been at least 550 shipwrecks on Superior. In 1913, between November 7 and 11, twelve ships went down with the loss of 250 mariners. And, probably because of Gordon Lightfoot's song, most everyone remembers the loss of the great ore ship *Edmund Fitzgerald* on November 10, 1975.

Recalling John Muir's excited cry as he ran out of his shelter during an earthquake shouting, "A noble earthquake," I decided to sally forth into the storm. Thoughts of deer hunting abandoned, I put on all the clothes I had and picked my way to the rocky shore. It was next to impossible to stand upright against the roaring wind or on the thick sheet of ice that was forming on the sandstone beach. I was forced to crawl back and cower behind a huge white pine tree to regain my footing.

There is an ancient and much higher shoreline cliff twenty yards behind the cabin. I scaled this former beach line and looked in awe at Lake Superior. All of its water, the entire 160 miles due north to Rossport, Canada, was roiling. Ten, fifteen foot waves crashed on the shore far below me. The gale force wind was driving snow horizontally.

No wonder the first nation peoples offered tribute to Mishipiizhhew, the powerful water spirit who dwelled in the lake, so he would calm the waves. The mariner's mantra crossed my mind: Even though Lake Superior seems to be enchanted, never, ever take the lake for granted.

Wet and cold, but deeply moved and energized by the power of the water, I decided to seek shelter in the huge caves just below where I stood. These caverns were carved by Lake Nipissing, the larger precursor of Lake Superior. The largest is more than 50 feet deep, 125 feet wide and more than eight feet tall at the entrance. It must have been a welcome shelter for Native Americans and early travelers.

Indeed, this big cave served as a Great Depression redoubt for a man I shall call Fred. A woods worker, day laborer and recluse, Fred lived here for almost two decades. One local resident described Fred as "not quite right in the head" and added that several men like him took to the woods during the economic hard times.

Fred had narrowed the entrance with evergreen boughs, now stripped of needles, and hung a blanket to keep out the cold winds. I built a small fire and looked around for remnants of his tenure in the cave. I found the remains of an old wood burning kitchen range (How did he get it in here?), two carbon-covered cooking pots and a rusty water dipper. Fred lived off the land—hunting, fishing and trapping for cash. He got by. Maybe the hermit of the cave was "right in the head" after all, I thought.

It was now late afternoon and, despite my small fire, I am chilled pretty thoroughly. I know exactly how to fix that: fire up the sauna. In short order the sauna stove is blazing. I throw some water on the rocks adorning the top of the stove and steam rises in delightful swirls. Now I am not only warmed but also feel very cleansed from inside out as I perspire copiously. Stress can't stand up to a hot sauna.

Should I go out au natural and roll in the snow? Why not? Making my way to the shoreline, I let the icy spray and snowflakes bombard my warm skin. And, I must confess, defied the Windigo by doing a brief version of the Dance of the Wild Cucumber in celebration of life.

When I returned—as swiftly as possible—to the sauna, I discovered a cluster of small, buff-colored moths clinging to the door. These small insects, the only living thing I saw the entire weekend, sport the amusing name of Linden Loopers (a.k.a. Winter moths) and they occur only in late fall. They prefer the leaves of basswood (linden) trees where the females—who are wingless—lay their eggs, ensuring a new generation the following year. All the moths clinging to the sauna door were males; their life's work done when they passed on their genes, they soon would die. But I had miles to go and I must get ready for the journey.

The woods and gales of November healed me thoroughly during my retreat. Not one thought about the client and his treatment still lingered in my mind. When I pulled into the driveway on Sunday evening, my wife, Lynn, noticed the difference instantly.

"I feel bully!" I blurted out to her unspoken question as to how I was. My bandage was no longer dirty.

William Hamilton

OLD FARMS

All about us in the U.P. are the footprints of our forebears: commercial fishing boats decaying on the shores of the Great Lakes; remnants of old logging camps deep in the forests; rusted old headframes of copper mines; large fallow fields slowly slipping back into woods.

Not long after moving to West Branch township southeast of Marquette, I became intrigued by the beautiful pastoral landscape. I was particularly drawn to the stalwart old barns I saw while exploring the country roads of our new home place.

Some tilt a bit, giving witness to the persistent pull of the earth and long congress with the prevailing winds. The passage of time, along with decades of rain, snow and summer sun are recorded on the faded wood siding. Yet these old barns have a heroic character. They have endured as have the people who wrested a living from the land. They are not dead relics but living lyrics singing quietly yet proudly of an earlier, simpler and physically demanding era.

Every year since then I go in late autumn to pay my respects to the farmers who toiled here long ago. I look in wonder at the size of the hay fields they wrested from the dense forest; I admire the craftsmanship of the ancient root cellars they built and marvel at the immense piles of rock they gathered from newly-plowed crop land.

PIONEER FARM IN WESTERN UPPER PENINSULA

On one of my annual journeys into a past era, I noticed an elderly man dressed in coveralls leaning on a fence post and gazing at a particularly immense field. EIdred Swanson was very appreciative—and somewhat bemused—about my interest in his old barn.

"The farming life could be rough—the weather always decided what type of crop you got," he reminisced after some urging. "But I'm glad I grew up back then. We knew who we were and what we had to do. It was very satisfying to rely on ourselves. We loved this land and it took care of us."

He trailed off, lost in memories, and looked away at his now-fallow fields. I edged away and pretended to take another photograph of his barn. As an erstwhile farm boy, I believe I know what he was thinking. How satisfying it is to sink tendrils deep into a place; how comforting it is to feel bonded to a particular landscape. Because of his long labors in his fields, the farmer had a personal connection to and reverence for the earth.

Most of the ancient barns stand empty now, their former tenants gone to other pastures. But if you listen closely, you may detect the faint lowing of cattle, the rattle of stanchions and the creak of wagons bringing hay to the barn in August. The smells, too, abide: the pungent richness of the lush hay fields, the virile smell of leather harnesses hanging on the walls, the pervasive aroma of cow manure.

There is a heroic symphony which flows from these old abandoned farms that those in a hurry or tethered to the distractions of modern technology do not hear or appreciate. What have we lost of our past with the passing of the family farm and the rise of industrial agriculture? Do we know where or how our food is raised? Can pig, chicken and cow factories really be good for us or the land?

My musing was interrupted by the ringing of Mr. Swanson's cell phone. He smiled ruefully at me as he pulled the phone from his coverall pocket. "The people at the assisted living home are checking on me again," he said with a deep sigh.

After a brief phone conversation, Eldred turned back to me and said, "Would you like this bloody thing?" I smiled and he continued, "Their intentions are good, I suppose, they just want to see the old farmer is okay, but sometimes it seems like I'm wearing one of those ankle tethers that parolees wear so the authorities can keep track of them. Well, I suppose I'll head back to town now. Hang around here if you want. No one in my family wants this old farm and when I croak—what the hell, I'm 91 years old—there'll be no one to watch over the home place."

"What was it like here in the old days?" I asked, before he could leave. What he said was almost an elegy for the pioneer farming way of life. I didn't write it down but what I remember is this:

> "I wish I could live it all again," he said. "We worked hard alright, but we still had more time for each other . . . the family as well as the neighbors. We always helped each other out with haying and such. There were gatherings for big feasts, card playing and joking around. Did you hear about the farmer who sold an old horse to a neighbor? The new owner took the horse home and less than an hour later it died. When the new owner confronted the farmer who sold him the horse, the farmer replied, 'Hmm, the horse never did that before.' We got a lot of amusement from simple stories like that. Most of us tried to accept nature as it is, not fighting it, but trying to blend into the land and the life it gave us."

After Eldred left, I wandered around the old homestead. The weathered buildings seemed to blend in and be in harmony with their surrounding, unlike the "look-at-me" school of architecture so prevalent now. That was when I got lost in a spasm of nostalgia.

At once autumn is both gloriously beautiful and deeply melancholy. As the earth tilts, the angle of the sun's rays sink lower, shadows become larger, darker. The creeping darkness and diminishing daylight reminds us that we, too, are temporary, transient residents on the earth and our lives are brief, hardly more than a tick of the cosmic clock.

I do not say this sadly or with any regrets. Indeed I smile at the youth within me who thought that life, at least his life, had no boundaries. Ah, but now the life-flame flickers a bit and I realize each day how precious the moments are. Without this faint awareness that life is finite, I am not sure humans would strive to seek, to find and not to yield. It requires a mature outlook and vigilance to live as fully as possible in the present moment.

So, I am glad to remember the correct medication for melancholy: I shall head to town and arrange a coffee and dessert date with one of my adopted granddaughters. Then the old memories of autumn and of life will ride more gently on my mind.

EPILOGUE: PILGRIM AT FOSTER CREEK

Life, I have found, is a wondrous adventure, an unfolding pilgrimage to be lived, not a problem to be solved. Along the way, I have been fortunate enough to discover bits of wisdom, some guidelines that helped me negotiate the peaks and valleys of my personal odyssey. I formulated these guidelines into ten fundamental principles—maxims—of how to conduct a wise and happy life.

Where did these ten maxims come from? I wish I could be sure. I think they were gleaned from several sources: life with a slow and halting tongue; many speech disabled persons with whom I have worked; a myriad of students who enriched my life on a daily basis; several mentors, both literary and personal; friends who shared the trail and lightened my load; and a healthy appreciation for serendipity.

A word of caution may be in order: These maxims, like this writer, are a work in progress. Be wary of anyone—most of all yourself— who has rigid assumptions about the way the world works. I keep these words by Andre Gide above my desk:

"Believe those who are seeking truth;

Doubt those who find it."

Watch out for "hardening of the categories," that dread disease of thinking whereby a mental groove becomes so wide and deep that you can't climb out of it.

Keep separate what you do for a living from who you are as a person.

Avoid building your life around one thing. In a prior lifetime, I was privileged to work as a university teacher of speech and hearing therapy. But I always took exception when someone referred to me as a speech therapist or worse, "the professor." That was my profession, not my identity. Why am I making this distinction? If we put all of our self-esteem into the work role basket, when things don't go well on the job, as sometimes they do not, the impact can be devastating.

So I encouraged my students to be complete persons, to dance, hike in the forest, listen to music and visit a museum. Whenever possible we abandoned the lecture hall and speech clinic for saunters and cookouts in remote places. The statute of limitations has expired so my confession is safe—we played hooky from the university, stealing time from our academic and clinical duties for psychic cleansing.

The students called these outings "mental hygiene days" and we rationalized that as laborers in the vineyard of speech therapy we must keep ourselves in better psychological health than our clients. You can't heal a wound with a dirty bandage—all of us from time to time become a bit soiled by the business of living.

In the process we relearned a basic truth: Nature extends wondrous healing powers to those willing to seek her surcease. On our woodland sojourns we discovered what Wordsworth meant when he wrote that the earth offers "a presence that disturbs our minds with the joy of elevated thought."

Remember the Law of the Echo.

Everything we do comes back to us. Our actions start a reaction like the ripples created when a stone is cast into a pond. The ripples move outward in ever larger circles, losing energy to be sure, but also making impacts on others in ways we often cannot know. He whose life I touch with my impact, touches others, and like a celestial game of billiards, the energy flows endlessly. Then, when we least expect it, the ripples can reappear on our personal shore in a refreshing eddy, and enrich our lives again.

If you can't change the facts, try adjusting your attitude.

Don't waste energy doing battle with conditions you cannot alter. Instead of obsessing upon the barrier, focus on what you *can* change; typically that involves looking at the situation from a different point of view.

During my university-era outings and now as the leader of nature hikes, I am continually amazed at the narrow range of comfort exhibited by some participants. A bit of rain, an uneven trail, temperatures deemed too hot or too cold, and a myriad of other conditions elicits complaints. Since I believe we should meet nature on its conditions, I am not very sympathetic to such lamenting.

Fortunately, my park ranger daughters taught me how to deal with whining. It's simple: *The leader whines first*. It works like this—let's say the path we are following takes a turn up a hill. The leader, in an exaggerated moaning voice, says, "Oh, nooo, you didn't say we were going to go up hill . . ." Typically, the participants look at each other in bemusement, grin and then keep whatever complaints they may have to themselves. Sic transit bellyaching!

Don't pole vault over mouse droppings.

How foolish it is to waste $100 worth of adrenaline on a ten-cent problem. But we all do it at times. When I get into a circumstance like that, I try to ask myself: If I get upset, will that help the situation? The Greek philosopher, Epictetus, observed in the first century that individuals are disturbed not by things or events but by their opinions of them. It is liberating to realize that I have a choice, that I am in charge and responsible for my reactions to events.

Don't wear your raincoat in the shower.

Life, it has been said, is not a dress rehearsal. Here and now, this is the life we have and the time we are given. It seems to me (with apologies to Thoreau) that many people lead lives of frantic desperation. They appear to skim over the surface of life, always running to catch up, complaining about lack of time for what they really want to do.

It takes a lot of self-discipline to live fully aware in the present moment. A walk in the woods can slow us down and help get us in tune with nature's rhythms. Try giving yourself up to the forest: focus on what you are seeing, hearing, smelling, as you saunter along. If you remember to leave the rest of your world at the trailhead, I can guarantee that you will return refreshed.

Let the craziness emerge at least once a day.

Mirth is good for both the soul and the body and adults need to do more of it. It matters not if others are not amused by our antics and admonish us to grow up. A zany sense of humor helped me get out of onerous committee assignments at the university. Realizing that the meetings were using up my time, I hit upon a method which would result in my removal from committee work. During a serious debate on some thorny academic issue, I interrupted the proceedings and inquired how a fly got on the ceiling. Did it buzz aloft and then suddenly turn over to land? Or did it crawl up the wall? The committee members looked at each other in bemusement if not alarm and my reputation was established: *Emerick does not work well on committees.* I smiled all the way back to the speech clinic.

Adventures in the outdoors encourage a playful attitude. You can hug a tree, try to embrace the wind, thank a white-throated sparrow for his lovely concert, do the Dance of the Wild Cucumber beside the Superior Lake. If you have forgotten how to be playful, invite some kids to go along. They know.

Prize those times when you are thwarted or frustrated.

Because you are blocked, you are then on the leading edge of creativity. Struggle is the law of growth and when someone is challenged, he or she must learn new strategies. A life without frustration is like a stew without seasoning. Bland.

I used to tell students during their supervised therapy practice that if they didn't make some mistakes, they weren't pushing the envelope hard enough. If you go through life thinking about the bad things that could happen, you soon convince yourself to do nothing.

Theodore Roosevelt's credo summarized this philosophy of aiming high in life:

"*Far better it is to dare mighty things, to win glorious triumphs, even though checkered by failure, than to take rank with those poor spirits who neither enjoy much nor suffer much, because they live in a gray twilight that knows not victory nor defeat."*

Strive to be a "there you are" rather than a "here I am" kind of listener.

We swim daily in an ocean of words. And despite the fact that we have two ears and consequently should listen twice as much as we talk, good listeners are an endangered species.

"Here I am" persons hear but don't really listen. They are simply waiting for their turn to talk. Although two persons seem to be in the conversation, "here I am" persons are really carrying on a serial monologue.

The "there you are" persons are good listeners. They really attend to and respond to what others are saying. They are seen as empathic, caring people and are sought out by others.

Keep looking for the pony.

Once upon a time, a team of psychologists was asked to discern why Ron and Don, ten-year-old twin brothers, were so different. Ron was a dour pessimist, while Don was determinedly cheerful and optimistic.

The psychologists isolated the brothers in two large rooms for almost an hour. First, the team looked to see what Ron was doing in his room, a large gymnasium filled with all sorts of new toys. The boy sat glumly beside the shiny playthings.

"Let's play with the ball and bat," suggested the psychologists.

"No, I would just lose," replied the pessimistic Ron.

"Well, here are some roller skates, how about trying them on?"

"No, I would just hurt myself," countered Ron.

Each time the team offered a new toy to the child, he responded with some glum or worried excuse.

Next, the psychologists entered Don's room, a large stall filled with manure. The child was ecstatic. He was leaping into the air, burrowing into the manure and laughing happily.

"Why are you so happy in this room filled with manure?" the psychologists asked.

Pausing only a moment, the optimistic twin replied: "With all this manure piled in the room, there just has to be a pony in here somewhere!"

Life is a journey, not a destination.

Although we may have good lovers and friends on the trip, we basically travel down life's pathway with ourselves. So it behooves us to strive to be the best companion we can be.

Let me say right away—I'm still a pilgrim finding my way. Still, showing more temerity than good sense, I cannot resist offering these working guidelines which are beacons in my own quest:

Treat yourself and everyone (and every thing) with respect

Seek simplicity, for it is complications which weigh us down and make the journey arduous

Practice joy, the simple delight of being alive in this wondrous planet

Strive for integrity: keep your word and be steadfast in your moral/ethical convictions

Honor the creative energy of life

One important aspect of a satisfying, whole life is a relationship with the earth. I am talking about a serious bonding with the natural features of your local area: identifying the watershed where you live; learning about the rocks and soil; celebrating the seasonal fragrances; learning the trees and flowers. Let the land bury itself deep in your heart.

There is, I think, a deep yearning in humans to touch the land, to feel the pulse of the earth. We remember somewhere deep in our memories that we are, despite our dazzling technological marvels, still creatures of the earth.

Each of us needs a listening point where we can reconnect and feel at one with the natural world. After years of searching, I have found the goal of my own pilgrimage here at our Foster Creek Homestead. I wish for you a special place—in the woods, by the water, in a park—a listening point from which to savor this precious Superior Peninsula.

CODE OF THE NORTH
An Open Letter to Prospective Immigrants

A longtime resident of the Upper Peninsula, disgruntled by the behavior of some summer visitors, composed a protest song. It is pretty blunt and a bit rude but you can judge for yourself. Here is the first verse:

> "We see you've reached the U.P., feast your ears and eyes,
> You just departed troll-land and aren't you surprised.
> You crossed the Mighty Mac and now you're over here,
> but this is not your playground, let's get that very clear."

In the spirit of more civil discourse, I was moved to prepare the following *Code of the North* so that visitors and would-be new immigrants to the Upper Peninsula would have a "user's manual" to guide them.

Code of the North

> "The Upper Peninsula requires prospective immigrants to struggle and endure its rigors before the land will accept them and bestow its blessings."
>
> Samuel Satterly, Copper Miner
Central Mine, 1875

It was one of those glorious evenings in August and the Upper Peninsula was putting on quite a show for a friend and prospective new resident.

We had taken our guest out to Little Presque Isle, a showplace of this area, for an evening stroll. The waves of the Superior Lake and the wind in the pines combined to create a wondrous natural symphony.

When we paused to admire the white-capped lake and the shadows in the slanting sun, a lone hermit thrush added his flute-like coda.

Even after all the years of enjoying this signature spot north of Marquette, Lynn and I were awestruck. Then our companion said, "Now, if only we could hear Bach playing in the background, this would be perfect."

We were astonished by his remark: Why were the natural sounds and visual beauty not enough?

As time goes on, more and more people will be coming north to seek the quality of life we enjoy—open space, opportunities for solitude, incredible beauty, availability of outdoor activities, a strong sense of heritage, lack of crowds, locally owned businesses, two-track roads, places where phones can't reach us—the list goes on.

Some new residents, however, may be hooked on romantic myths about the north, much more so than longtime residents. Far more alarming, they have false expectations about bringing their urban/suburban lifestyles into the great outdoors.

There is an unwritten code of conduct, usually respected by people living in the Upper Peninsula. To be sure, the wild of the north has been tamed. Consider the oxymoronic slogan developed by an out-of-state consulting firm and adopted a few years ago by an area tourist association to lure people here: "Discover how civilized our wilderness can be."

Fortunately for those of us addicted to wild places and natural settings, there still are large tracts of forest to tramp, undeveloped rivers to fish and a myriad of sparkling clean lakes to swim or launch a boat.

However, before seeking admission to this Superior Peninsula, a newcomer will want to be aware of the realities of living in the isolated north country; it presents very different challenges than urban or suburban life.

That is why we like it, and we harbor some anxiety that new residents or visitors will arrive with certain expectations of comfort that lead them to try to alter what we love.

Climate

Actually, we don't have a climate in the U.P., we have weather. Do we ever have weather! There is no way to gloss it over: we have long, cold, snowy winters.

In order to survive and thrive here, you have to be able to find positive values in the lengthy white season. (Have you ever spent time looking—really looking—at snowflakes, or long blue shadows in January?) Finding joy in winter here also requires strong inner resources to use the time to learn and entertain oneself.

Insects

Blackflies, wood ticks, mosquitoes, deer flies. These critters descend in hordes as soon as the snow melts. Don't expect massive spraying programs here.

Wildlife

There are bears in the woods (and sometimes in town), deer on the roads (and sometimes eating plants in your yard), a thriving population of timber wolves and lots of other smaller animals. It's their home, too, and they were here first.

Roads

There is no interstate highway in the U.P., except for one short section from the Mackinac Bridge to Sault Ste. Marie. Most of the roads are two-lane. There are many miles of gravel and two-track dirt roads to explore.

If you choose to build your home in a remote area, don't expect the roads to be paved, the school bus to trundle out for your children, water and septic service to be provided, electric wires to be strung to your new location or the snowplow to show up early on the morning after the big January storm. Rural living is what it is, and is likely to remain so.

Transportation

Some planes, no trains, mostly cars for moving about up here. Be aware that weather is a major factor in both flying and driving; it takes more time to get somewhere and sometimes you can't get there from here.

Phones

There are places in this region where a cell phone will not work. Many of us think that's a good thing, as we view the proliferation of tall, visible towers needed to carry those signals.

Emergencies

Keep in mind that the population is sparse and the distances are great, so it may take longer for a first responder corps or an ambulance crew to reach you in the event of an accident or sudden illness.

Consumer items

Although the region is well on its way to possessing every chain superstore known to Western civilization, there may be items or choices that frustrate the urban-dweller or longtime lover of gigantic malls.

Employment

The options for gainful employment you may have enjoyed in more populous areas will be much more limited here. Even if you are lucky enough, or creative enough, to put together satisfactory work here, you may have to be willing to trade the high salaries of the cities for other values to be gained.

As a longtime lover of this wondrous Superior Peninsula, I worry what the future may bring. The slower pace of life and the gentle rhythms of the land are part of our being. Will visitors or prospective immigrants embrace the whole experience of living in the Upper Peninsula and add their enthusiasm, creativity and skills to the community, or will they come with other, more material values and attempt to alter us as well as the land? Will we morph into a venue, not a place—a backdrop for activities and ways of living that one could do anywhere?

I offer only this plea:

Please don't come to the Upper Peninsula and try to alter the land or our way of life. Don't set about to change this place into the place you have just left (or fled).

It is what it is, and we like it that way.

Rather, approach our beloved north country with reverence and awe.

Tuck yourself in here and let the land change you.

Acknowledgment to: *Code of the West,* published by Gallatin County, Montana

ACKNOWLEDGEMENTS

No writer is an island and many persons offered valuable assistance during the gestation of this book:

Pat Ryan O'Day, publisher of the *Marquette Monthly,* has been an enthusiastic cheerleader for decades. We have been privileged to author articles and a monthly column, from which several of the essays included in *Paradise North* are drawn. The *MM* is an indispensable publication to many of its readers in the Upper Peninsula and elsewhere.

Mark Mitchell, George Wanska, Dean Premo, Evan Premo and *Lynn Emerick* graciously gave permission to include their photographs as highlights for this book. Their images have made vivid the people and places of Upper Peninsula.

The illustration skills of *William Hamilton* and *Carolyn Damstra* have been most valuable in carrying out the themes envisioned for the book.

Jack Deo of Superior View Studio, Marquette, provided photographic scanning services with cheerful expertise.

Steve Schmeck of www.manytracks.com, once again performed his much-appreciated bar code magic.

Lynn Emerick, my longtime editor and life-partner, somehow has made sense of all my scribbling and helped to bring this book to life with her usual attention to detail.

And for all the readers and booksellers who asked, "When is the next U.P. book coming?" Here it is.

Photo credits and locations *(for your exploring pleasure)*

Front cover images:
Summer on Lake Superior, Alger County: Lon Emerick
Eben Ice Caves - Rock River Wilderness, Hiawatha National Forest: Lon Emerick
Trillium at AuTrain: Lynn Emerick
Autumn at Harlow Lake: Lynn Emerick

Back cover images:
Author photo, McLain State Park: Lynn Emerick
Emerging ferns, South Marquette: Lon Emerick
Lake Superior - Wetmore Landing, Little Presque Isle Natural Area: Lon Emerick
Autumn on the Middle Branch, Escanaba River: Lynn Emerick

Winter section
Ice rounds in Lake Superior, Wetmore Landing: Mark Mitchell
Ice spray, Window in Marquette home: Mark Mitchell
Eben Ice Caves: Lon Emerick
Forest shadows, Rock River Wilderness: Lon Emerick

Spring section
Marsh marigolds, Laughing Whitefish Falls Scenic Site: Lon Emerick
Spring birches, Mt. Marquette: Lon Emerick
Grand Island Overlook Roadside Park, Munising: Lynn Emerick
Point Iroquois Lighthouse, Chippewa County: Lynn Emerick
Showy Ladyslippers - near Trout Lake, Alger County: Lon Emerick

Summer section
Little Presque Isle, from Freeman's Landing: Mark Mitchell
Sundew - Lake Superior shoreline, Alger County: Lon Emerick
Lake Camp - Lake Superior, AuTrain: Lon Emerick
Fishing at Pinnacle Falls - Yellow Dog Plains, Marquette County: Evan Premo

Autumn section
High point near Sugar Loaf Mountain, north toward Little Presque Isle:
    Mark Mitchell
Storm over Lake Superior, looking north toward Little Presque Isle: Mark Mitchell
Fall collage - Carp River, south of Mt. Marquette: Mark Mitchell
Goldenrod, any fall roadside: Lon Emerick

Other books from North Country Publishing

Sharing the Journey — Lessons from my Students and Clients with Tangled Tongues

Going Back to Central (Mine) — On the Road in Search of the Past in Michigan's Upper Peninsula

Lumberjack — Inside an Era in the Upper Peninsula of Michigan

The Superior Peninsula — Seasons in the Upper Peninsula of Michigan

You Wouldn't Like it Here — A Guide to the Real Upper Peninsula

You STILL Wouldn't Like it Here — The Sequel

1-866-942-7898
www.northcountrypublishing.com